1-MINUTE
Bible
GUIDE

180 KEY NAMES
OF GOD

Your Key to Understanding

BARBOUR BOOKS
An Imprint of Barbour Publishing, Inc.

© 2020 by Barbour Publishing, Inc.

ISBN 978-1-64352-286-9

All rights reserved. No part of this publication may be reproduced or transmitted for commercial purposes, except for brief quotations in printed reviews, without written permission of the publisher.

Churches and other noncommercial interests may reproduce portions of this book without the express written permission of Barbour Publishing, provided that the text does not exceed 500 words and that the text is not material quoted from another publisher. When reproducing text from this book, include the following credit line: "From *1-Minute Bible Guide: 180 Key Names of God*, published by Barbour Publishing, Inc. Used by permission."

All scripture quotations, unless otherwise noted, are taken from the King James Version of the Bible.

Scripture quotations marked NIV are taken from the HOLY BIBLE, NEW INTERNATIONAL VERSION®. NIV®. Copyright © 1973, 1978, 1984, 2011 by Biblica, Inc.™ Used by permission. All rights reserved worldwide.

Scripture quotations marked HCSB are taken from the Holman Christian Standard Bible ® Copyright © 1999, 2000, 2002, 2003, 2009 by Holman Bible Publishers. Used with permission by Holman Bible Publishers, Nashville, Tennessee. All rights reserved.

Scripture quotations marked NASB are taken from the New American Standard Bible, © 1960, 1962, 1963, 1968, 1971, 1972, 1973, 1975, 1977, 1995 by The Lockman Foundation. Used by permission.

Scripture quotations marked NRSV are taken from the New Revised Standard Version Bible, copyright 1989, Division of Christian Education of the National Council of the Churches of Christ in the United States of America. Used by permission. All rights reserved.

Scripture quotations marked NLT are taken from the *Holy Bible*. New Living Translation copyright© 1996, 2004, 2015 by Tyndale House Foundation. Used by permission of Tyndale House Publishers, Inc. Carol Stream, Illinois 60188. All rights reserved.

Published by Barbour Books, an imprint of Barbour Publishing, Inc., 1810 Barbour Drive, Uhrichsville, Ohio 44683, www.barbourbooks.com

Our mission is to inspire the world with the life-changing message of the Bible.

Member of the
Evangelical Christian
Publishers Association

Printed in the United States of America.

CONTENTS

Introduction...9
Abba, Father.. 11
Advocate 12
Alive for Evermore 13
All, and in All 14
Almighty God... 15
Alpha and Omega 16
Amen...17
Ancient of Days......................................18
Anointed...19
Apostle 20
Author and Finisher of Our Faith 21
Beginning of the Creation of God 22
Beloved Son..23
Bread... 24
Breath of the Almighty...............................25
Bridegroom 26
Bright and Morning Star..............................27
Captain of Salvation 28
Chief Cornerstone 29
Chosen of God...................................... 30
Christ... 31
Christ Crucified......................................32
Comforter 33
Consolation of Israel................................ 34
Consuming Fire......................................35
Counsellor 36
Creator 37
Daysman.. 38
Dayspring from on High..............................39
Deliverer.. 40

Desire of All Nations. 41
Door 42
Dwelling Place. 43
End of the Law. 44
Eternal Life. 45
Eternal Spirit 46
Everlasting Father. 47
Everlasting God. 48
Express Image of God. 49
Faithful and True 50
Father of Glory 51
Father of Lights. 52
Father of Mercies 53
Father of Our Lord Jesus Christ 54
Father of Spirits. 55
Firstbegotten. 56
Firstborn from the Dead 57
Firstfruits 58
Forerunner 59
Fortress. 60
Foundation 61
Fountain of Living Waters 62
Free Spirit. 63
Friend of Publicans and Sinners 64
Fullers' Soap. 65
Gift of God. 66
Glory of Israel 67
God 68
God of Abraham, Isaac, and Jacob 69
God of All Comfort. 70
God of Gods. 71
God of Heaven. 72
God of My Salvation 73

God of Peace 74

God of the Whole Earth 75

God Who Sees 76

Good Master 77

Good Shepherd 78

Good Spirit 79

Governor 80

Great High Priest 81

Great Prophet 82

Guide unto Death 83

Head of All Principality and Power 84

Head of the Church 85

Head of the Corner 86

Heir of All Things 87

Hiding Place 88

High Priest after the Order of Melchisedec 89

Holy One 90

Holy Spirit of God 91

Hope of Glory 92

Horn of My Salvation 93

Husband 94

I Am 95

I Am That I Am 96

Immanuel / Emmanuel 97

Jehovah 98

Jehovah-Jireh 99

Jehovah-Nissi 100

Jehovah-Shalom 101

Jesus 102

Judge of All the Earth 103

Judge of Quick and Dead 104

Just Man 105

Keeper 106

King Eternal, Immortal, Invisible 107

King of Glory 108

King of Kings 109

King of the Jews 110

Lamb of God 111

Last Adam 112

Lawgiver 113

Life 114

Light of Israel 115

Light of the World 116

Lion of the Tribe of Judah 117

Living God 118

Living Stone 119

Lord 120

Lord God of Israel 121

Lord of Hosts 122

Lord of Peace 123

Lord of the Dead and Living .124

Lord of the Harvest 125

Lord of the Sabbath 126

Lord Our Righteousness 127

Lord Over All 128

Lord Who Heals 129

Lord Who Sanctifies 130

Majesty on High 131

Maker 132

Man of Sorrows 133

Master 134

Mediator 135

Messiah 136

Mighty One of Jacob 137

Minister of the True Tabernacle 138

Most High 139

New Spirit 140
One Chosen Out of the People 141
Only Begotten Son 142
Only Wise God 143
Our Passover 144
Physician 145
Portion 146
Potter 147
Power of God 148
Power of the Highest 149
Prince of the Kings of the Earth 150
Propitiation for Our Sins 151
Rabbi 152
Redeemer 153
Refiner's Fire 154
Refuge 155
Resurrection and the Life 156
Righteous Servant 157
Rock 158
Root and Offspring of David 159
Saviour 160
Sceptre Out of Israel 161
Seed of the Woman 162
Seven Spirits 163
Shepherd 164
Shield 165
Shiloh 166
Son of Abraham 167
Son of David 168
Son of God 169
Son of Man 170
Son of Mary 171
Son Over His Own House 172

Spirit of Adoption 173

Spirit of Faith 174

Spirit of Glory 175

Spirit of Knowledge and the Fear of the Lord 176

Spirit of Life 177

Spirit of Prophecy 178

Spirit of Truth 179

Spirit of Wisdom and Revelation 180

Spiritual Rock 181

Star Out of Jacob 182

Strength 183

Strong Tower 184

Teacher Come from God 185

Truth 186

Vine 187

Wall of Fire 188

Way 189

Word 190

Better biblical understanding—in about one minute per entry.

Everyone could use a better grasp of scripture—and the 1-Minute Bible Guide series offers you just that. This easy-to-read book covers the 180 most important names and titles of God the Father, Jesus Christ, and the Holy Spirit, offering a representative verse and a concise description that can be read and digested in 60 seconds or less. And, if you want to dig deeper, most entries include additional references for further study.

Over the course of these entries—read straight through or one per day like a devotional—you'll gain a clearer view of the all-powerful, all-loving, all-amazing God we serve. Get better biblical understanding—in about one minute per entry.

ABBA, FATHER

And he said, Abba, Father, all things are
possible unto thee; take away this cup from me:
nevertheless not what I will, but what thou wilt.
MARK 14:36

This is the name with which Jesus the Son addressed God the Father in His agonizing prayer in the garden of Gethsemane. *Abba* is an Aramaic word of affection for "Father," similar in meaning to "Papa" in the English language.

The Jewish people generally avoided such affectionate terms for God. They thought of Him as an exalted and larger-than-life being who demanded respect. He was to be spoken of in hushed reverence rather than addressed as if He were a member of the family.

But it was appropriate for Jesus to address the Father as *Abba*. As God's Son, He knew the Father more intimately than anyone has ever known Him. Jesus Himself declared, "As the Father knoweth me, even so know I the Father" (John 10:15).

Through His death on the cross, Jesus made it possible for us to know God as a loving, forgiving Father. The apostle Paul declared, "And because ye are sons, God hath sent forth the Spirit of his Son into your hearts, crying, Abba, Father" (Galatians 4:6).

Learn More: Matthew 6:9 / Mark 9:7 / Luke 10:21 / John 3:35; 10:37–38

ADVOCATE

*My little children, these things write I
unto you, that ye sin not. And if any
man sin, we have an advocate with
the Father, Jesus Christ the righteous.*

1 JOHN 2:1

This is the only place in the Bible where Jesus is called by this name. It expresses the idea that He stands before God on our behalf. He serves as our "defense attorney" to represent us before the Father in heaven when Satan, the accuser, charges us with sin. Jesus' argument on our behalf is solid because it is based on His own atoning work—His death on the cross for our sins.

Any attorney will tell you that his client must be totally honest about the charges that have brought him into court. Unless the advocate knows everything about the circumstances of the case, he cannot represent his client adequately before the judge and jury.

In the same way, if we expect Jesus to serve as our Advocate before God, we as believers must be honest with Him when sin creeps into our lives. Full disclosure, also known as confession, is essential. As the apostle John wrote, "If we confess our sins, he is faithful and just to forgive us our sins, and to cleanse us from all unrighteousness" (1 John 1:9).

Learn More: Romans 10:9 / 1 John 4:15

ALIVE FOR EVERMORE

I am he that liveth, and was dead; and,
behold, I am alive for evermore, Amen;
and have the keys of hell and of death.

REVELATION 1:18

These words are among the first that Jesus spoke when He revealed Himself to the apostle John on the isle of Patmos. This revelation occurred about fifty or sixty years after Jesus' death and resurrection. He assured John that He was not only alive but "alive for evermore."

During His brief ministry of about three years, Jesus predicted His death and resurrection on more than one occasion (Matthew 16:21–28; Mark 10:32–34; Luke 9:43–45). But even His disciples had a hard time believing this would happen.

Even after Jesus appeared to them in His resurrection body, they had doubts. To prove that they were not seeing a ghost or a vision, Jesus encouraged the disciples to touch His hands and feet, showing that He had flesh and bones. He even ate a piece of fish and a honeycomb as they looked on, confirming that He had a physical body just like theirs (Luke 24:37–43).

Since Jesus experienced a physical resurrection and is alive for evermore, we as believers have His assurance that death is not the end of life but a glorious new beginning.

Learn More: Acts 1:3 / 1 Thessalonians 4:17

ALL, AND IN ALL

*Where there is neither Greek nor Jew,
circumcision nor uncircumcision,
Barbarian, Scythian, bond nor free:
but Christ is all, and in all.*
COLOSSIANS 3:11

Jesus was born into a divided world. Jews looked down on Gentiles. Greeks considered themselves superior in education and culture to the Jews. But the apostle Paul declared in this famous passage that the coming of Jesus changed all that. He is the "All in All"—the great unifier—who brings all people together at the foot of the cross.

To those who know Jesus, worldly distinctions and social status are no longer important. The only thing that really matters is Christ. He is the sum and substance of life—the absolute and the center of our existence. Because He gave His all to purchase our salvation, our purpose in life is to bring honor and glory to Him. As Jesus expressed it in His Sermon on the Mount, "Let your light so shine before men, that they may see your good works, and glorify your Father which is in heaven" (Matthew 5:16).

Learn More: Matthew 28:19–20 / Acts 10:34–35 / Romans 3:29 / Ephesians 4:4–6

ALMIGHTY GOD

And when Abram was ninety years old
and nine, the LORD appeared to Abram,
and said unto him, I am the Almighty God;
walk before me, and be thou perfect.
GENESIS 17:1

God had already promised Abram (later renamed Abraham) that He would make his descendants a great nation and give them a land of their own (Genesis 12:1–3; 13:15–17). But Abraham had no son through whom this promise could be fulfilled. The Lord, by identifying Himself as "the Almighty God" in this verse, declared to Abraham that He had the power to make this happen.

The Hebrew words behind this divine compound name also express the idea of plenty. Some interpreters suggest that they may be rendered as "the All-Sufficient One" or "the All-Bountiful One." God not only has the power to bless His people, but He *will* do so abundantly. The apostle Paul put it like this: God is "able to do exceeding abundantly above all that we ask or think" (Ephesians 3:20).

Learn More: Psalm 45:3 / Isaiah 1:24; 49:26 / Jeremiah 32:18 / 2 Corinthians 6:18 / Revelation 15:3; 19:6

ALPHA AND OMEGA

*I am Alpha and Omega, the beginning
and the end, the first and the last.*
REVELATION 22:13

This is one of four places in the book of Revelation where Jesus is called by this name (see also 1:8, 11; 21:6). In all four places, Jesus uses this name of Himself.

The alpha and the omega were the first and last letters of the Greek alphabet—the language in which most of the New Testament was originally written. Thus this name is a poetic way of declaring that Jesus is the beginning and the end of all things. We might put it this way in modern terms: "Jesus is the A and Z of life and everything in between."

No letter stands before the alpha, and no letter follows the omega. This shows that Jesus defines truth and reality. All other gods that people worship are counterfeit deities. He encompasses all things and rejects all limitations.

Jesus also declared that He is the "first and the last" (Revelation 1:17)—a name that means basically the same thing as Alpha and Omega. As the first, He was present with God the Father before the creation (John 1:2). In the last days, He will bring the world to its appointed end (Revelation 22:10–12). See also *Beginning of the Creation of God.*

Learn More: Revelation 2:8

AMEN

*And unto the angel of the church of the
Laodiceans write; These things saith
the Amen, the faithful and true witness,
the beginning of the creation of God.*

REVELATION 3:14

This verse was spoken by Jesus as He prepared to deliver a special message to the church at Laodicea. By designating Himself as "the Amen," He claimed to be speaking a truthful, authoritative word for this church.

The word *amen* has a rich biblical history. In the Old Testament, it was used to confirm an oath or consent to an agreement. For example, Nehemiah called on the people of his time not to cheat and defraud one another. The people responded with "amen" to pledge their agreement with his proposal (Nehemiah 5:13).

Jesus often used the word *verily* (or *amen*) in His teachings to show that He was about to speak God's words of truth (Matthew 16:28). In modern translations, this Greek word is rendered as "Truly I tell you" (NIV) or "I assure you" (HCSB). The early church used *amen* to declare "let it be so" or "let it be true" at the close of prayers (2 Thessalonians 3:18), just as we do today.

Because Jesus is the great Amen, we can trust His words and His leadership. He is the sum and substance of truth (John 14:6). He will never say or do anything that will cause us to stumble or go astray. He has promised that if we follow Him, we will know the truth, and this truth will make us free (John 8:32).

Learn More: 1 Kings 1:36 / Jeremiah 28:6 / Romans 16:20

ANCIENT OF DAYS

*I beheld till the thrones were cast down,
and the Ancient of days did sit, whose garment
was white as snow, and the hair of his head
like the pure wool: his throne was like the fiery
flame, and his wheels as burning fire.*

DANIEL 7:9

This name of God is used only by the prophet Daniel (see also 7:13, 22). He had a vision of four world empires that rose to great power and prominence, only to eventually fall and crumble into insignificance.

In contrast to the short life of these world powers was One who had always existed and always would. Daniel's use of the imagery of old age to describe God suggests His eternality. Unlike humans and worldly affairs, God is not limited by time. Everything around us changes, but He remains the same. The only real security we have in this world is to place our trust in the Ancient of Days.

"King of old," a title used by the psalmist (Psalm 74:12), expresses basically the same idea about God.

Learn More: Genesis 21:33 / Deuteronomy 33:27 / Psalm 90:2 / Isaiah 40:28 / Habakkuk 1:12

ANOINTED

The kings of the earth set themselves,
and the rulers take counsel together,
against the Lord, and against his anointed,
saying, Let us break their bands asunder,
and cast away their cords from us.
PSALM 2:2–3

Psalm 2 is a "messianic psalm," one that predicts the coming of the Messiah. Rebellion against the Lord by the nations of the world is futile, the psalmist declared, because God has appointed Christ, "his anointed," as the King of the earth.

This name of Jesus reflects the anointing custom of the Old Testament. Priests and kings were anointed by having oil poured on their heads. This ritual showed that a person had been especially chosen or set apart to perform the responsibilities of his office.

As God's anointed, Jesus Christ was set apart for His role as the divine mediator and redeemer. Through Him we find forgiveness for our sins and the abundant life that God intends for His people.

Jesus in turn has anointed us as believers for the task of declaring His message of hope in a desperate world. The apostle Paul put it like this: "We are therefore Christ's ambassadors, as though God were making his appeal through us. We implore you in Christ's behalf: Be reconciled to God" (2 Corinthians 5:20 NIV).

Learn More: Leviticus 8:10–12 / 1 Samuel 16:13 / Luke 4:18

APOSTLE

Wherefore, holy brethren, partakers of the heavenly calling, consider the Apostle and High Priest of our profession, Christ Jesus; who was faithful to him that appointed him, as also Moses was faithful in all his house.
HEBREWS 3:1–2

Jesus selected twelve apostles (Mark 3:14; 6:30) to learn from Him and to carry on His work after He was gone. But here Jesus Himself is called "the Apostle." This is the only place in the Bible where this name of Jesus occurs.

The basic meaning of the word *apostle* is a person sent on a special mission with delegated authority and power. Jesus sent out the Twelve to teach and heal, and He gave them the ability to succeed in this mission (Mark 6:7–13). They continued this teaching and healing ministry even after Jesus' resurrection and ascension to the Father (Acts 2:38–43).

But Jesus was the ultimate Apostle. Under the authority of His Father, He came into the world on a mission of love and grace. He did not falter in His task. From the cross He declared triumphantly, "It is finished" (John 19:30). His provision for our salvation was complete, but the Good News about His death and resurrection—the Gospel—rolls on across the ages.

Learn More: Matthew 10:2 / Acts 4:33 / Ephesians 2:20

AUTHOR AND FINISHER OF OUR FAITH

*Looking unto Jesus the author and finisher of our
faith; who for the joy that was set before him
endured the cross, despising the shame, and is
set down at the right hand of the throne of God.*
HEBREWS 12:2

Jesus is called "author" in this verse from Hebrews, as well
as in Hebrews 5:9: "And being made perfect, he became
the author of eternal salvation unto all them that obey him."
In one modern translation, He is also called "the author of
[our] salvation" (Hebrews 2:10 NASB).

An author is someone who creates. Jesus is the author
of our faith or salvation in that He has provided us with
the only flawless example of what the life of faith is like.
The New Revised Standard Version expresses this idea by
calling Him the "pioneer" of our faith. He blazed the trail
for all others who seek to follow His example.

But Jesus not only *started* the journey—He brought it
to *completion* as the "finisher" ("perfecter," NRSV) of faith.
He did not stop until He guaranteed our final redemption,
making it possible for us to enjoy eternal life with Him in
heaven.

Learn More: John 19:30 / Hebrews 10:12

BEGINNING OF THE CREATION OF GOD

And unto the angel of the church of the
Laodiceans write; These things saith
the Amen, the faithful and true witness,
the beginning of the creation of God.
REVELATION 3:14

The affirmation of this verse is that Jesus has always been. Before He was born into the world in human form, He existed with God the Father. The Nicene Creed, a famous statement of faith formulated by the church in AD 325, put it like this: "I believe in one Lord, Jesus Christ. . .born of the Father before all ages." Thus He is called the "beginning of the creation of God."

Not only has Jesus existed eternally; the Bible affirms that He participated with God in the creation. On the sixth day of creation the Lord declared, "Let us make man in *our* image, after *our* likeness" (Genesis 1:26, emphasis added). The plural *our* probably refers to God in His trinitarian existence: God the Father, God the Son, and God the Holy Spirit.

This creative force in the universe has promised that believers will live with Him in eternity. The apostle Paul declared, "we have a building from God, an house not made with hands, eternal in the heavens" (2 Corinthians 5:1).

Learn More: Genesis 1:1 / John 1:1–3 / Colossians 1:16–17 / Ephesians 3:9

BELOVED SON

*And Jesus, when he was baptized, went
up straightway out of the water. . .and he
saw the Spirit of God descending like a
dove, and lighting upon him: and lo a voice
from heaven, saying, This is my beloved
Son, in whom I am well pleased.*
MATTHEW 3:16–17

In graphic terms, these verses describe what happened when Jesus was baptized by John the Baptist at the beginning of His public ministry. The heavens opened, the Holy Spirit settled on Jesus, and God identified Him clearly as His "beloved Son" who brought Him joy. God was pleased with Jesus because He had waited patiently on the Father's timing. Now Jesus was ready to begin the work for which He had been sent into the world.

God the Father repeated these words near the end of Jesus' public ministry following His transfiguration (Matthew 17:1–5). His words on this occasion showed He was pleased with what His beloved Son had done. Only Jesus' death and resurrection to follow could top the divine work He had already accomplished.

Because Jesus was God's beloved Son, we as believers in Jesus are also known as the Father's beloved (Romans 1:7). We hold a special place in His heart because we have been cleansed by Jesus' blood and are committed to the work of His everlasting kingdom.

Learn More: Matthew 3:17 / Luke 9:35 / 2 Peter 1:17

BREAD

*Then Jesus said unto them, Verily, verily,
I say unto you, Moses gave you not that
bread from heaven; but my Father giveth
you the true bread from heaven.*
JOHN 6:32

John 6 might be called the "bread chapter" of the New Testament. In this long narrative, Jesus uses four different names for Himself involving the imagery of bread: "bread from heaven" (verse 32), "bread of God" (verse 33), "bread of life" (verse 35), and "living bread" (verse 51).

Bread made from wheat or barley was the staple food of Jesus' day, so the common people could identify with these names. Bread was also closely identified with some of the major events from Israel's history. When the Israelites left Egypt in the Exodus, they baked their bread without leaven because they didn't have time to wait for the bread to rise (Exodus 12:30–34). The Lord also kept His people alive in the wilderness after the Exodus by providing manna, a bread substitute, for them to eat (Numbers 11:6–9).

Just as God provided food in the wilderness, He also provides spiritual sustenance for His people. As the living bread and the bread of life, Jesus provides eternal life for those who claim Him as their Lord and Savior.

Learn More: Matthew 26:26 / Luke 22:19 /
1 Corinthians 10:17

*The spirit of God hath made me, and the breath
of the Almighty hath given me life.*
JOB 33:4

This name of the Holy Spirit comes from the long speech
that the young man Elihu addressed to Job. He spoke after
Job's three friends—Eliphaz, Bildad, and Zophar (Job 2:11)—
had ended their speeches.

Elihu stated that he owed his life to the breath of God.
This is a reference to God's creation of the first man in the
garden of Eden. The Lord "breathed into his nostrils the
breath of life; and man became a living soul" (Genesis 2:7).
It was God's own breath that brought Adam to life. Even
today, our ability to inhale life-giving oxygen into our lungs
is evidence of God's care of the physical world through the
agency of His Spirit.

The Holy Spirit, or the "breath of the Almighty," also
energizes believers in a spiritual sense. Just before His
ascension to the Father, Jesus empowered His followers
to carry on His work by breathing on them and charging
them to receive the Holy Spirit (John 20:22). This is the
same life-giving Spirit that enables believers in our time to
witness to others about God's transforming power.

Learn More: Job 4:9 / Psalm 33:6 / Isaiah 42:5 /
Daniel 5:23 / Acts 17:25

BRIDEGROOM

*And Jesus said unto them, Can the children
of the bridechamber mourn, as long as the
bridegroom is with them? but the days will
come, when the bridegroom shall be taken
from them, and then shall they fast.*

MATTHEW 9:15

Jesus responded with these words when the followers of John the Baptist asked why He and His disciples did not participate in the ritual of fasting. His answer picked up imagery from a Jewish wedding, with Jesus referring to Himself as the bridegroom and His disciples as the wedding guests.

It would not be appropriate, Jesus said, for His disciples to fast or mourn while He as the bridegroom was physically present with them. They should save their fasting for the time after His death and resurrection, when Jesus would be taken up to heaven by God the Father.

Perhaps Jesus was looking ahead to the birth of the church, which is spoken of symbolically as His bride (Revelation 21:9). The apostle Paul pointed out that just as "the husband is the head of the wife," so "Christ is the head of the church" (Ephesians 5:23). Jesus loved the church so much that He laid down His life for it (Ephesians 5:25). Every single member of His kingdom has experienced this sacrificial love.

Learn More: Luke 5:34–35 / Revelation 21:2

BRIGHT AND MORNING STAR

I Jesus have sent mine angel to testify
unto you these things in the churches.
I am the root and the offspring of David,
and the bright and morning star.
REVELATION 22:16

This is one of the last names of Jesus mentioned in scripture, since it appears in the final chapter of the last book of the Bible. How appropriate that He should call Himself the "bright and morning star," a name associated with a heavenly body and its light.

The people of ancient times did not know as much about stars and planets as we know today. To them the last star to disappear in the eastern sky as the sun began to rise was known as the "morning star." Astronomers of modern times have identified this "star" as the planet Venus, earth's closest neighbor. Because of its closeness, Venus is the third brightest object in the sky, outshone only by the sun and the moon.

When the light from all the other stars disappeared in the early morning, this star shone on, signaling the beginning of a new day. The birth of Jesus also marked the beginning of a new day, a truth that should bring joy to our hearts. What better way to greet the dawning of each new day than to breathe a prayer of thanks to God for sending His bright and morning star into the world?

Learn More: Numbers 24:17 / Matthew 2:2 / 2 Peter 1:19 / Revelation 2:27–28

For it became him, for whom are all things,
and by whom are all things, in bringing many
sons unto glory, to make the captain of their
salvation perfect through sufferings.
HEBREWS 2:10

This is the only place in the Bible where Jesus is called by this name. The Greek word behind *captain* in this verse is rendered as "author" in Hebrews 12:2. Other meanings of this word are "prince" and "leader."

This verse from Hebrews goes on to say that Jesus was made "perfect through sufferings." A genuine leader does not ask his followers to do something that he is not willing to do himself. He sets the example for those he leads. This is what Jesus did when He died on the cross for us. We as believers will never suffer more by following Him than He did to make it possible for us to be cleansed of our sins.

A leader also guides, encourages, inspires, and motivates the people in his charge. We can rest assured that we are in good hands when we follow our captain of salvation.

Learn More: Psalm 48:14 / Isaiah 63:5 / John 16:13 / Hebrews 1:14

CHIEF CORNERSTONE

Now therefore ye are no more strangers and
foreigners, but fellow citizens with the saints,
and of the household of God; and are built upon
the foundation of the apostles and prophets,
Jesus Christ himself being the chief corner stone.
EPHESIANS 2:19–20

With these words the apostle Paul assured believers in the church at Ephesus that they were recipients of God's grace. Their faith in Christ had brought them into God's kingdom, because He was the "chief corner stone" on which this kingdom was built.

This image is rooted in a famous messianic passage that was written several centuries before Jesus was born. In Psalm 118:22, the psalmist declared, "The stone which the builders refused is become the head stone of the corner."

Jesus identified with this passage during the final days of His ministry. He knew that He would be rejected as the Messiah by His own people. So he told the disciples that His offer of salvation would pass to the non-Jewish (Gentile) nations that would accept Him as Lord and Savior (Matthew 21:42–43).

In the stone buildings of Bible times, a cornerstone was used to hold two opposing rows of stones together at the point where they came together in a corner. Jesus as the chief cornerstone is the force on which our faith is based. Though He may be rejected by the nonbelieving world, He is our hope in this life and the life to come.

Learn More: Isaiah 28:16 / Mark 12:10 / Acts 4:11 /
1 Peter 2:7

CHOSEN OF GOD

And the people stood beholding. And the
rulers also with them derided him, saying,
He saved others; let him save himself,
if he be Christ, the chosen of God.
LUKE 23:35

Religious leaders and other people around the cross called Jesus by this name as He was dying. The irony is that their ridicule was a perfect description of Him and the divine mission from His Father that brought Jesus into the world.

For generations the Jewish people had looked for a messiah who would deliver God's people. Jesus was that chosen one, but He was not the type of champion they expected. He came not as a military conqueror but as a spiritual savior who died to rescue people from their sin. His work as the "chosen of God" continues to this day as He calls people to follow Him (Matthew 16:24).

Jesus was the chosen of God in a special sense. But He followed in the tradition of many people in the Bible who were said to be chosen of God. These included the descendants of Jacob, also called the Israelites (1 Chronicles 16:13), King Solomon (1 Chronicles 29:1), Moses (Psalm 106:23), Zerubbabel (Haggai 2:23), the apostle Paul (Acts 9:15), and all believers (Ephesians 1:4).

Learn More: Psalm 33:12 / Isaiah 42:1 / Matthew 12:18 / 1 Peter 2:4, 9

CHRIST

*And Simon Peter answered and said, Thou
art the Christ, the Son of the living God.*
MATTHEW 16:16

This verse is part of the account of Peter's confession of
Jesus as the Messiah (or "anointed one") in the Gospel of
Matthew (16:13–20). Peter declared that Jesus was the
anointed one, a special agent who had been sent into the
world by God Himself. He was the Son of God, the Messiah,
the great deliverer for whom the Jewish people had been
looking for many years.

Jesus commended Peter for recognizing Him as God's
anointed. But He went on to caution the disciples not
to tell anyone "that he was Jesus the Christ" (Matthew
16:20). He probably gave this command because the Jewish
people expected their messiah to be a military and political
champion. Jesus could not live up to these expectations
because He was a spiritual messiah. He had been sent to
teach about the kingdom of God, to heal the sick, and to
deliver the people from their sin. He would eventually
reveal Himself as the Messiah (Luke 22:70–71), but only
after He had completed the spiritual mission on which
He had been sent.

Because Jesus was the anointed one of God, we as His
followers are also commissioned to continue His work in
the world (2 Corinthians 1:21–22).

Learn More: Luke 9:20 / Romans 3:24 / 1 Corinthians 1:2

CHRIST CRUCIFIED

But we preach Christ crucified,
unto the Jews a stumblingblock,
and unto the Greeks foolishness.

1 CORINTHIANS 1:23

This is the only place in the Bible where this name of Jesus appears. The word *Christ* means "the anointed one" or "the messiah," so the literal meaning of the name is "the messiah crucified."

In Jewish tradition, the coming messiah was to be a powerful leader who would defeat all their enemies and rule over a restored Israel. That this messiah would die on a Roman cross like a common criminal was something they found totally unacceptable—a "stumblingblock" that prevented them from accepting Jesus as the Messiah.

A crucified Savior who died in our place to set us free from bondage to sin is still a foreign concept to many people. Like the rich young ruler of Jesus' day, they want to know "what good thing" (Matthew 19:16) they must do to obtain eternal life. But there is nothing we can do that will buy God's favor. We must accept by faith the provision that God has already made for our salvation through the death of His Son.

The apostle Paul put it like this: "For by grace are ye saved through faith; and that not of yourselves: it is the gift of God: not of works, lest any man should boast" (Ephesians 2:8–9).

Learn More: Matthew 27:35 / Acts 2:36 / Galatians 2:20

COMFORTER

*And I will pray the Father, and he shall
give you another Comforter, that he
may abide with you for ever.*
JOHN 14:16

Jesus spoke these words after He had told the disciples that His death was drawing near. He would no longer be with them in a physical sense, but He was not leaving them alone: He would send a "Comforter," the Holy Spirit, to fill the void caused by His return to the Father in heaven after His resurrection.

Jesus referred to the Holy Spirit as "another" Comforter. The Greek word He used means "another of the same kind." Jesus Himself was the chief Comforter of His disciples, and He was sending another like Himself to serve as His stand-in. So close and personal would be the presence of the Holy Spirit that it would seem as if Jesus had never left.

The Greek word behind Comforter is *parakletos*, meaning "one called alongside." This is the same word translated as "Advocate," another name of Jesus (1 John 2:1).

When Jesus promised that the Comforter will come "alongside" us, He meant that the Holy Spirit will help us in our times of need. His presence will sustain us through the tough times of life.

Learn More: Isaiah 40:1 / John 14:26; 15:26; 16:7 / Acts 9:31

CONSOLATION OF ISRAEL

And, behold, there was a man in Jerusalem,
whose name was Simeon; and the same
man was just and devout, waiting for
the consolation of Israel.
LUKE 2:25

Shortly after Jesus was born, Joseph and Mary took Him to the temple in Jerusalem to be dedicated to the Lord. A man named Simeon was moved by the Holy Spirit to come to the temple at the same time. He immediately recognized the infant Jesus as the "consolation of Israel."

The word *consolation* means "comfort" or "relief." In the Old Testament, God had promised that He would send His Messiah to His people. Simeon was convinced that he would not die before he had seen this come to pass. God apparently showed Simeon by divine revelation that the baby Jesus was the fulfilment of this promise.

This good news had a dark side, though. Simeon went on to tell Mary and Joseph that many people would accept their Son as the Messiah but many would not. He also revealed to Mary that "a sword shall pierce through thy own soul also" (Luke 2:35)—a hint of Jesus' future crucifixion.

Jesus' birth was good news for those who accepted His messiahship and bad news for those who refused to believe in Him. The task of Christians is to help others find the consolation that Jesus can bring into their lives.

Learn More: Job 15:11 / Romans 15:5 / 2 Thessalonians 2:16 / Hebrews 6:18

CONSUMING FIRE

Wherefore we receiving a kingdom which cannot be moved, let us have grace, whereby we may serve God acceptably with reverence and godly fear: for our God is a consuming fire.
HEBREWS 12:28–29

God is often associated with fire in the Bible. Sometimes fire symbolizes His guidance and protection. For example, He spoke to Moses from a burning bush (Exodus 3:2). He guided the Israelites through the wilderness at night by a pillar of fire (Exodus 13:21).

But this verse from the book of Hebrews shows that fire is also a symbol of God's wrath. To those who are disrespectful or disobedient, He is a searing flame of judgment. For example, when the Israelites complained against Moses in the wilderness, God sent His fire of judgment upon the troublemakers (Numbers 11:1–3). Years earlier, He also rained fire and brimstone from heaven against the evil people of the cities of Sodom and Gomorrah (Genesis 19:24)

All people must decide for themselves whether the Lord will be a guiding light or a consuming fire in their lives. See also *Wall of Fire.*

Learn More: Numbers 26:10 / Deuteronomy 5:24–25 / 1 Kings 18:38 / Psalm 21:9

COUNSELLOR

For unto us a child is born. . .and his name shall
be called Wonderful, Counsellor, The mighty God,
The everlasting Father, The Prince of Peace.
ISAIAH 9:6

This verse is probably the most familiar messianic prophecy in the book of Isaiah. It is especially quoted at Christmastime when believers gather to celebrate the birth of Jesus.

The word *counsel* refers to guidance, advice, or instruction. The Bible is filled with models of good and bad counsel and counselors who fall into both of these categories.

For example, on the good side, Daniel provided wise counsel to an aide to King Nebuchadnezzar of Babylon, after the king had issued an order to have all his wise men put to death (Daniel 2:10–16). But on the foolish side, King Rehoboam of Judah rejected the wise counsel of the older leaders of the nation and listened to the foolish counsel of his young associates (1 Kings 12:6–8). This led to the rebellion of the northern tribes and the division of the united kingdom of Solomon into two separate nations (1 Kings 12:16–19).

We can depend on Jesus, our wise Counsellor, to always provide us with good instruction. He guides us with grace and righteousness. He will never give us bad advice that would cause us to go astray.

Learn More: Psalm 73:24 / Proverbs 19:21 / Isaiah 11:2

*Hast thou not known? hast thou not heard, that the everlasting God, the L*ORD*, the Creator of the ends of the earth, fainteth not, neither is weary? there is no searching of his understanding.*

ISAIAH 40:28

The prophet Isaiah was amazed that the people of Judah were rejecting the one true God and worshiping false gods instead. The Creator God had brought the universe into being by the power of His word (Hebrews 11:3). These pagan idols were weak and puny by comparison.

From the first chapter of the Bible we learn several important truths about God's creation of the world and its inhabitants. (1) He created the world from nothing; He is the ultimate cause of all that exists. (2) The creation was accomplished in orderly fashion, in six successive days. This means that God has placed order and design into the universe. (3) Man is the crown of God's creation. (4) The Lord has given us the responsibility to take care of His world.

As Isaiah reminded the people of his nation, the one-and-only Creator God is solely worthy of our loyalty and worship. See also *Maker.*

Learn More: Ecclesiastes 12:1 / Romans 1:22–25 / 1 Peter 4:19

DAYSMAN

Neither is there any daysman betwixt us,
that might lay his hand upon us both.
JOB 9:33

This verse is part of Job's complaint that God was punishing him without cause. Job was convinced that he had done nothing to deserve his suffering. To make matters worse, God was all-powerful and Job was simply a weak human being. Job had no right to question God, so he longed for a daysman—a referee, mediator, or impartial judge—who could speak to God on his behalf.

Job's desire for someone to represent him before God the Father was eventually fulfilled with the coming of Jesus Christ into the world. As the God-man, He is fully human and fully divine. He communicates directly with the Father, because He is God's Son. But He identifies with us humans in our frailties because He came to earth in human form.

It's difficult for us to comprehend how Jesus could be both human and divine at the same time. But our lack of understanding doesn't make the fact untrue. The apostle Paul attempted to explain it like this: Although Jesus was equal with God and had the nature of God, He emptied Himself of these divine attributes to become a man who was "obedient unto death, even the death of the cross" (Philippians 2:8).

Learn More: Job 8:3 / Psalm 72:2; 89:14 / Isaiah 9:7; 33:22

DAYSPRING FROM ON HIGH

Through the tender mercy of our God; whereby
the dayspring from on high hath visited us.
LUKE 1:78

This verse is part of a passage in the Gospel of Luke known as the "Benedictus" (Luke 1:68–79)—a prayer uttered by Zacharias, after the birth of his son, John the Baptist. An angel had revealed to Zacharias before John's birth that the boy would become the forerunner of the Messiah. Zacharias praised God for sending the Messiah, Jesus, whom he called the "dayspring from on high."

The English term *dayspring* comes from a Greek word that means "a rising up." It is generally used to describe the rising of the sun in the morning and the appearance of stars in the night sky. Thus Zacharias thought of Jesus the Messiah as a bright light that God was preparing to send into a dark world.

The words *on high* reveal the origin of this dayspring. Jesus did not come into the world on His own as a solitary agent. He was on a mission of redemption from God the Father.

The prophet Malachi used a similar name for Jesus in his prophecy about the coming Messiah. He called Him the "Sun of righteousness" who would "arise with healing in his wings" (Malachi 4:2).

Learn More: Job 38:12 / Psalm 84:11

DELIVERER

And so all Israel shall be saved: as it is written,
There shall come out of Sion the Deliverer,
and shall turn away ungodliness from Jacob.
ROMANS 11:26

In this verse the apostle Paul referred to a portion of Psalm 14:7. This is a messianic psalm attributed to David, who declared that the salvation of God's people would come from Zion, or Jerusalem.

This is an unusual reference to the Messiah, because Jesus was born in Bethlehem, not Jerusalem. But Jesus was crucified and resurrected in Jerusalem. This is also the place where the church was born on the day of Pentecost (Acts 2:1–41) following Jesus' ascension. These facts are probably what Paul had in mind when he declared that Jesus as our Deliverer came out of Jerusalem.

God is also referred to in the Old Testament as our Deliverer. This was one of King David's favorite words for God, perhaps because God had delivered him from danger many times throughout his life (1 Samuel 18:10–11; 19:11–12).

As Deliverer, the great work that Jesus performs is rescue from sin. He sets us free from our sin that separates us from God (Isaiah 59:2). He delivers us from the power of Satan, who temps us constantly to fall back into sin (Ephesians 6:11–13). And He will deliver His followers from a world filled with sin when He returns to claim us as His own.

Learn More: 2 Samuel 22:2 / Psalm 18:2; 31:2; 40:17

*And I will shake all nations, and the desire
of all nations shall come: and I will fill this
house with glory, saith the L*ORD* of hosts.*

HAGGAI 2:7

The prophet Haggai spoke these words to the Jewish exiles who had returned to Jerusalem after their period of captivity in Babylonia and Persia. He challenged them to get busy with the task of rebuilding the Jewish temple that had been destroyed several decades before by the invading Babylonian army. The temple is apparently the "house" referred to in this verse.

But Haggai's words looked beyond his time to the distant future when Israel's Messiah would become the "desire of all nations." At Jesus' return in glory in the end time, all nations will pay Him homage and recognize His universal rule throughout the earth. One modern translation renders this name as the "wealth of all nations" (NASB).

Jesus is not only the desire of believers, He is the hope of the entire world. As the apostle Paul declared, "At the name of Jesus every knee should bow. . .every tongue acknowledge that Jesus Christ is Lord, to the glory of God the Father" (Philippians 2:10–11 NIV).

Learn More: Psalm 22:27; 72:17 / Isaiah 11:10 / Matthew 28:19 / Galatians 3:8 / Revelation 7:9

DOOR

*I am the door: by me if any man
enter in, he shall be saved, and shall
go in and out, and find pasture.*
JOHN 10:9

This is one of several "I Am" statements of Jesus in the Gospel of John. A door is an opening or entryway into a building or a shelter. By affirming that He was the door, Jesus made it clear that He was the only way to salvation and eternal life.

In His sermon on the mount, Jesus also addressed this topic by talking about two gates (Matthew 7:13–14). The broad gate, representing the way of the world, was so wide that people could drift through it without any conscious thought about what they were doing. But the narrow gate, representing Jesus and His teachings, required commitment and sacrifice from those who wanted to enter this way and follow Him.

Maybe you have heard people say, "It doesn't matter what you believe as long as you're sincere," or "All religions are basically the same; they just take us to heaven by different paths." Don't believe it. Jesus declared, "I am the way, the truth, and the life: no man cometh unto the Father, but by me" (John 14:6).

Learn More: John 10:7–8 / Acts 4:12

DWELLING PLACE

*Lord, thou hast been our dwelling
place in all generations.*
PSALM 90:1

This psalm may be the oldest in the entire book of Psalms, since it is attributed to Moses (see psalm title). He led the Israelites during their years of wandering in the wilderness. This was before they settled in Canaan, so they lived in tents and moved from place to place.

It's interesting that Moses would call God the people's "dwelling place" at a time when they did not have permanent homes. In spite of their primitive living arrangements, they still thought of God as their ultimate dwelling place. His presence followed them wherever they moved, and His faithfulness continued from one generation to the next.

When the psalmist considered the Lord's promise to protect His people, he declared, "There shall no evil befall thee, neither shall any plague come nigh thy dwelling" (Psalm 91:10). God is still a dwelling place for His people. Whether we live in an apartment, a mobile home, a condominium, a gated community, or a mansion, we find in Him all the joys and comforts of home.

Learn More: Psalm 4:8; 23:6; 91:1 / 2 Corinthians 5:1 / Revelation 21:3

END OF THE LAW

*For Christ is the end of the law for
righteousness to every one that believeth.*
ROMANS 10:4

This is the only place in the Bible where Jesus is referred to by this name. The New International Version clarifies the meaning of this verse by stating that He is the "culmination of the law so that there may be righteousness for everyone who believes." This name of Jesus has a double meaning.

First, Jesus is the end of the law because He did everything required by the Old Testament law to become a righteous person. He lived a sinless life and obeyed all of God's commandments, although He was tempted to do wrong, like any person in a human body (Hebrews 4:15).

Second, Jesus is the end of the law because He brought an end to law-keeping as the way for people to find justification in God's sight. Belief in Jesus as Lord and Savior is the only way to deal with sin and eliminate the separation that exists between God and man.

Some things outlive their usefulness and ought to be brought to an end or transformed into something better. We should be grateful that Jesus—as the end of the law—offers all believers a glorious new beginning.

Learn More: Jeremiah 31:31–33 / Romans 6:14 /
Galatians 2:16 / Hebrews 7:19

ETERNAL LIFE

*And we know that the Son of God is come,
and hath given us an understanding, that we
may know him that is true, and we are in him
that is true, even in his Son Jesus Christ.
This is the true God, and eternal life.*
1 JOHN 5:20

In several places in the New Testament, Jesus is described as the provider of eternal life. For example:

- "The gift of God is eternal life through Jesus Christ our Lord" (Romans 6:23).
- "This is the promise that he hath promised us, even eternal life" (1 John 2:25).
- "Looking for the mercy of our Lord Jesus Christ unto eternal life" (Jude 21).

But this verse from 1 John is the only place in the Bible where Jesus Himself is given the name *eternal life*. The apostle John was probably thinking about the resurrection of Jesus, His ascension to the Father, and His declaration, "I am alive for evermore" (Revelation 1:18).

Jesus tasted death like all mortal human beings. But He was gloriously raised and restored to His place of honor with God the Father in heaven. As the perfect model of eternal life, He promises that all who place their trust in Him will live in eternal fellowship with Him.

Learn More: John 3:16; 17:3 / 1 Corinthians 15:22 / 1 John 2:25

ETERNAL SPIRIT

*How much more shall the blood of Christ,
who through the eternal Spirit offered himself
without spot to God, purge your conscience
from dead works to serve the living God?*

HEBREWS 9:14

The Holy Spirit empowered Jesus throughout His public ministry. Jesus was led by the Spirit into the region of Galilee, where He began to teach and heal (Luke 4:14). Jesus cast demons out of people "by the Spirit of God" (Matthew 12:28). And this verse from the book of Hebrews shows that the Holy Spirit—described here as "the eternal spirit"—gave Jesus the strength to offer His life as a sacrifice for sin.

This is the only place in the Bible where the phrase "eternal spirit" appears. It clearly identifies the Holy Spirit as a divine being. Only the three persons of the Trinity— Father, Son, and Holy Spirit—are eternal. Everything else is created matter.

The eternality of the Holy Spirit is evident in the very first book of the Bible. As God began to mold and shape the universe, "the Spirit of God moved upon the face of the waters" (Genesis 1:2). Thus, the Spirit existed with God before time began and participated with Him in the creation of the world.

Learn More: Job 33:4 / Psalm 33:6; 104:30 / John 14:26 / Acts 2:1–3

EVERLASTING FATHER

*For unto us a child is born. . .and his name shall
be called Wonderful, Counsellor, The mighty
God, The everlasting Father.*

ISAIAH 9:6

We are accustomed to making a distinction between God
and Jesus by referring to God as the Father and to Jesus
as the Son. But in this famous passage, the prophet Isaiah
seems to blur these neat lines by referring to *Jesus* as "The
everlasting Father."

This name of Jesus shows the dilemma we face in trying
to explain the Trinity, or God's existence in three different
modes or essences—Father, Son, and Holy Spirit.

Some people explain the Trinity by using the analogy
of water. We know that water is one substance, but it can
exist in three different forms—liquid, ice, and vapor. In the
same way, so this analogy goes, God exists in the three
different modes known as the Trinity—one substance in
three different forms.

Rather than resorting to analogies like this, we are better
off if we admit that there is no rational way to explain the
Trinity. Faith takes over where reasoning ends. Jesus was
separate from God but one with Him at the same time
because He Himself declared: "I and my Father are one"
(John 10:30).

Learn More: Genesis 21:33 / Isaiah 40:28 / Romans 16:26

EVERLASTING GOD

*And Abraham planted a grove in
Beersheba, and called there on the
name of the LORD, the everlasting God.*
GENESIS 21:33

Abraham had moved from place to place for several years in the land of Canaan, the territory that God had promised to his descendants (Genesis 12:1–5). Finally, the patriarch decided to make a site known as Beersheba the center of the territory where he would graze his flocks and herds. Here Abraham dug a well and planted a grove of trees to mark the site as his permanent dwelling place.

At Beersheba it was appropriate that Abraham should call on the name of "the everlasting God," the One without beginning and end who would never cease to be. He would guide Abraham into the future and fulfill His promise that Abraham's offspring would eventually populate this entire region.

God kept His promise, but it took a while. More than five centuries would pass after Abraham's time before the Israelites conquered the land and made it their own.

We should remember that the everlasting God never gets in a hurry; He is not limited by time as we humans are.

Learn More: Psalm 90:1–2 / Isaiah 40:28 / Romans 16:26

EXPRESS IMAGE OF GOD

Who being the brightness of his glory, and the express image of his person, and upholding all things by the word of his power, when he had by himself purged our sins, sat down on the right hand of the Majesty on high.

HEBREWS 1:3

This name occurs at the beginning of the book of Hebrews, where the writer declared that Jesus is the climax of God's revelation of Himself. In the past He had communicated to His people through the prophets, but now He has "spoken unto us by his Son" (Hebrews 1:2).

The Greek word behind "express image" refers to engravings in wood, impressions in clay, or stamped images on coins. The word picture implies that Jesus was an exact duplicate of His Father in His attitudes, character, and actions. Physical features are not included in this resemblance, because God is a spiritual being (John 4:24).

This name tells us that Christ perfectly represents God His Father. If we want to know what God is like, we should examine the life and ministry of His Son.

Have you ever heard someone say, "That boy is just like his father"? Sometimes, because of a youngster's bad behavior, this pronouncement can cause embarrassment for a father. But God was always pleased with the actions of His Son (Luke 3:22).

Learn More: 2 Corinthians 4:4 / Colossians 1:15

FAITHFUL AND TRUE

Behold a white horse; and he that sat upon him was called Faithful and True, and in righteousness he doth judge and make war.
REVELATION 19:11

In this verse near the end of the book of Revelation, the heavens were opened and the apostle John saw Jesus. The white horse on which He was seated symbolized His triumph over all His enemies. As the "Faithful and True," Jesus was coming to earth in judgment against unrighteousness and injustice.

This verse contains images that are similar to the portrayal of God as the divine judge in the Old Testament. The psalmist looked forward to the time when God would judge the earth with righteousness and its people with His truth (Psalm 96:13). Since God is the standard of truth, He has the right to set the standards by which the world will be judged.

God has delegated to His Son the authority to judge the world. Jesus is faithful to God's promise of judgment, and He is the true One who will judge by God's standard of ultimate truth.

In an unjust and unrighteous world, we have to admit that truth does not always win out. But the final work of judgment belongs to Him who is called Faithful and True.

Learn More: 1 Corinthians 1:9 / 2 Thessalonians 3:3 / 1 John 1:9 / Revelation 3:14

FATHER OF GLORY

*That the God of our Lord Jesus Christ, the
Father of glory, may give unto you the spirit of
wisdom and revelation in the knowledge of him.*
EPHESIANS 1:17

This is the only place in the Bible where God is called "the Father of glory." The apostle Paul used this name while assuring the believers at Ephesus that he was praying to the Father on their behalf.

The word *glory* appears many times throughout the Bible, usually in reference to God's splendor, moral beauty, and perfection. At times His glory was revealed visibly—for example, shortly after the construction of the tabernacle and temple (Exodus 40:34; 1 Kings 8:11). Jesus' glory or splendor was revealed in a special way at His transfiguration before His disciples Peter, James, and John (Matthew 17:2).

The prophet Isaiah declared of the Lord, "The whole earth is full of his glory" (Isaiah 6:3). To put it another way, the beauty and majesty of the physical world gives evidence of God's presence in His creation.

Just as God is the Father of glory, believers should bring glory to Him by becoming living examples of His goodness in the world.

Learn More: Isaiah 28:5 / Matthew 16:27 / Acts 7:2 / Romans 6:4

FATHER OF LIGHTS

*Every good gift and every perfect gift
is from above, and cometh down from
the Father of lights, with whom is no
variableness, neither shadow of turning.*
JAMES 1:17

With this name of God, James probably had in mind the creation account in the book of Genesis. On the fourth day of creation God created the sun, moon, and stars and "set them in the firmament of the heaven to give light upon the earth" (Genesis 1:17).

The pagan people of many ancient cultures thought of the heavenly bodies as gods. But James declared that they were created things, brought into being by the one true God of the universe. Only the "Father of lights" is worthy of worship.

This God who created the light-giving bodies of the heavens is also dependable and trustworthy. As the New International Version translates it, He "does not change like shifting shadows." God's presence is an unwavering light that guides His people through this life and beyond.

Those who follow the Lord should carry His light as a witness to others. The apostle Peter declared "Ye are a chosen generation. . .that ye should shew forth the praises of him who hath called you out of darkness into his marvellous light" (1 Peter 2:9).

Learn More: Genesis 1:3 / Isaiah 2:5 / John 8:12 /
2 Corinthians 4:6

FATHER OF MERCIES

*Blessed be God, even the Father of
our Lord Jesus Christ, the Father of
mercies, and the God of all comfort.*
2 CORINTHIANS 1:3

This is another of the apostle Paul's names for God that appears in only one verse in the Bible. In this case, he used "Father of mercies" in his prayer for the believers in the church he founded at Corinth.

The dictionary defines *mercy* as "compassionate treatment of those in distress." Because of the original disobedience of Adam and Eve in the garden of Eden, humankind is caught in a web of sin. But we can be grateful that God refuses to abandon us in this perilous situation.

If the Lord gave us what we deserved, we would be destitute and lost. But His love and patience won't let us go. God the Father sent His Son, Jesus, into the world to deliver us from our sin. This is the supreme example of His mercy and love.

Because God is the originator—or Father—of mercies, He expects His people to show this attribute of His character to others. Jesus declared, "Be ye therefore merciful, as your Father also is merciful" (Luke 6:36).

Learn More: Deuteronomy 4:31 / Psalm 86:15; 136:2 / Micah 6:8 / 1 Peter 1:3

FATHER OF OUR LORD JESUS CHRIST

We give thanks to God and the Father of
our Lord Jesus Christ, praying always for you,
since we heard of your faith in Christ Jesus,
and of the love which ye have to all the saints.
COLOSSIANS 1:3-4

This name of God used by the apostle Paul draws attention to the miraculous birth of Jesus the Son. He did not have a human father but was miraculously conceived in the womb of Mary by God the Father, acting through the Holy Spirit (Luke 1:34-35).

Jesus was sent by God to fulfill the Father's work of redemption in the world. When He was only twelve years old, Jesus stated that this was His divine mission (Luke 2:48-49). His declaration from the cross, "It is finished" (John 19:30), shows that He accomplished the purpose for which He was sent—our salvation.

This verse is one of several in the New Testament in which these three names of Jesus—*Lord*, *Jesus*, and *Christ*—appear in succession. This happens especially in the book of Acts and the writings of the apostle Paul. He urged the Christians at Rome to "glorify God, even the Father of our Lord Jesus Christ" with "one mind and one mouth" (Romans 15:6).

Learn More: Acts 16:31; 20:21; 28:31 / Romans 1:7 / 1 Corinthians 1:3 / Galatians 6:14

FATHER OF SPIRITS

Furthermore we have had fathers of our flesh which corrected us, and we gave them reverence: shall we not much rather be in subjection unto the Father of spirits, and live?
HEBREWS 12:9

This is one of those places in the Bible where the addition of one word makes all the difference in its meaning. Rather than "Father of spirits," the New Living Translation renders this name of God as "Father of *our* spirits" (emphasis added). This rendering makes it clear that the writer of Hebrews was contrasting physical fathers ("fathers of our flesh") with God as our Father in a spiritual sense.

Earthly fathers discipline their children, teaching them right from wrong and respect for others. God our spiritual Father teaches us to obey Him as the ultimate authority, to follow His commands, and to present our lives as living sacrifices for His honor and glory. The next verse in the New International Version says our fathers "disciplined us for a little while as they thought best; but God disciplines us for our good, in order that we may share in his holiness" (Hebrews 12:10).

Most fathers admit they are far from perfect, but the heavenly Father is an always-right, never-failing guide and provider. "In all thy ways acknowledge him," the writer of Proverbs declared, "and he shall direct thy paths" (Proverbs 3:6).

Learn More: Matthew 5:45; 6:8 / Luke 11:2 / John 6:32 / Romans 8:15

FIRSTBEGOTTEN

And again, when he bringeth in the
firstbegotten into the world, he saith,
And let all the angels of God worship him.
HEBREWS 1:6

The word *he* in this verse refers to God the Father, and *firstbegotten* refers to His Son, Jesus Christ. But because Jesus has existed from eternity with the Father, how could He be the firstborn or "firstbegotten into the world"?

The term refers to Jesus' incarnation, or His appearance in human flesh. True, He has existed with the Father from the beginning. But there was a specific point in time when He was conceived by the Holy Spirit in Mary's womb and then born nine months later like any human infant (Luke 1:35; 2:7). This is one sense in which the title "firstbegotten" is applied to Jesus.

The word also refers to rank or order. To say that Jesus is God's firstbegotten is to declare that He ranks above all other beings except the Father Himself. This verse from Hebrews makes the point that Jesus is higher than all of God's angels, because they are told to bow down and worship Him.

As God's firstbegotten (or firstborn), Jesus is worthy of our honor and praise. The apostle Peter declared that all believers should glorify Jesus Christ, "to whom be praise and dominion for ever and ever" (1 Peter 4:11).

Learn More: Psalm 89:27 / Romans 8:29 / Colossians 1:15

FIRSTBORN FROM
THE DEAD

And he is the head of the body, the church:
who is the beginning, the firstborn from
the dead; that in all things he might
have the preeminence.
COLOSSIANS 1:18

The apostle Paul applied this name to Jesus in his description of Jesus as head of the church. "Firstborn from the dead" expresses basically the same meaning as the name "first begotten of the dead" (Revelation 1:5).

This name refers to Jesus' resurrection. But in what sense was He the "firstborn from the dead"? Jesus was not the first person in the Bible to be brought back to life following physical death. The prophet Elisha raised a boy back to life (2 Kings 4:18–37). Jesus Himself raised three people from the dead: the daughter of Jairus (Matthew 9:18–26), the son of a widow in the village of Nain (Luke 7:11–15), and His friend Lazarus (John 11:41–44).

But all these resurrections were temporary stays of death. These people eventually died again. Jesus rose from the grave, never to die again. He was the first person to overcome death and to appear in a glorified body (Luke 24:36–39). Jesus has the authority and power to provide bodily resurrection and eternal life for all who commit their lives to Him (1 Corinthians 15:12–26).

Learn More: Romans 8:29 / Colossians 1:15

FIRSTFRUITS

*But now is Christ risen from the dead, and
become the firstfruits of them that slept.*
1 CORINTHIANS 15:20

This name of Jesus occurs in the apostle Paul's famous passage about the resurrection of Jesus and His promise of a similar resurrection for all believers (1 Corinthians 15:12–57). Paul based his argument for Jesus' resurrection on the fact that He had been seen by many other believers during the days after He rose from the dead (1 Corinthians 15:3–7). He was the "firstfruits" of the resurrection, the model that had blazed the trail for others.

The Jewish people thought of the firstfruits (the first of their crops to be gathered) as God's harvest. These were presented as offerings to God on the day of the firstfruits, a part of the celebration of the festival known as Pentecost (2 Chronicles 31:5).

To Paul, Jesus through His resurrection was the firstfruits of a spiritual harvest known as eternal life. Believers were the rest of the harvest that would be gathered in at the appointed time. Just as Jesus had been raised from the dead to reign with His Father in glory, so their bodies would be "raised incorruptible" (1 Corinthians 15:52) at His second coming, and they would live with Him forever in heaven.

Learn More: Leviticus 23:10 / Proverbs 3:9 /
1 Corinthians 15:23 / Revelation 14:4

FORERUNNER

*Whither the forerunner is for us entered,
even Jesus, made an high priest for ever
after the order of Melchisedec.*
HEBREWS 6:20

A forerunner is an advance agent, the lead person on a team. He goes ahead on a scouting mission to spot possible dangers and prepare the way for others who will follow. Good examples of forerunners in the Bible are the twelve spies sent by Moses to investigate the land of Canaan (Numbers 13:1–3) and the forerunner of Jesus, John the Baptist (Mark 1:1–8).

But the ultimate forerunner, according to the author of Hebrews, was Jesus Christ Himself. He came to prepare the way so we could become citizens of God's kingdom. Following His death and resurrection, He returned to His Father in heaven (Acts 1:9). Here He has prepared a place for us. We as believers have His word that we will live there with Him forever. "If I go and prepare a place for you," He promised, "I will come again, and receive you unto myself; that where I am, there ye may be also" (John 14:3).

Learn More: Genesis 45:5–7 / Luke 1:76

FORTRESS

O LORD, my strength, and my fortress,
and my refuge in the day of affliction.
JEREMIAH 16:19

A fortress was any heavily fortified place that provided protection from enemy attacks. In Bible times, a defensive wall around a city, with reinforced towers and gates, was considered the ultimate fortress.

In this verse Jeremiah portrayed the Lord as his fortress. The prophet's unpopular message that Judah would fall to its enemies subjected him to ridicule, imprisonment, and charges of treason. At the beginning of Jeremiah's ministry, God promised that He would make him "a defenced city, and an iron pillar, and brasen walls against the whole land" (Jeremiah 1:18). The Lord had made good on His promise.

A phrase in the Bible that means basically the same thing as fortress is "strong hold." The prophet Nahum declared: "The LORD is good, a strong hold in the day of trouble; and he knoweth them that trust in him" (Nahum 1:7).

Like these two prophets, all of us need a fortress or stronghold at times. This advice from Peter can help us persevere when troubles seem to fall like the spring rain: "Cast all your anxiety on him because he cares for you" (1 Peter 5:7 NIV). See also *Strong Tower.*

Learn More: 2 Samuel 22:2 / Psalm 91:2 / Jeremiah 16:19

FOUNDATION

For other foundation can no man lay
than that is laid, which is Jesus Christ.
1 CORINTHIANS 3:11

In his first letter to the believers at Corinth, the apostle Paul dealt with divisions in the church (1 Corinthians 1:10–15). The people were following four different authority figures—Paul, Apollos, Cephas, and Christ. Paul made it clear in this verse (3:11) that the one foundation on which they should be basing their faith was Jesus Christ.

Jesus Himself addressed this issue during His earthly ministry. In the parable of the two foundations, He described men who built houses on different sites (Matthew 7:24–27). The house built on sand collapsed in a storm. But the second house stood firm in violent weather because "it was founded upon a rock" (verse 25).

The message of this parable is that almost any foundation will do when the weather is good. But only a faith based on the solid foundation known as Jesus Christ can withstand the gales and floods of life.

Several centuries before Jesus was born, the prophet Isaiah looked ahead to the coming of the Messiah and referred to Him as the "sure foundation" (Isaiah 28:16).

Learn More: Job 4:19 / Psalm 16:8 / Ephesians 2:20

FOUNTAIN OF LIVING WATERS

For my people have committed two evils;
they have forsaken me the fountain of living
waters, and hewed them out cisterns,
broken cisterns, that can hold no water.
JEREMIAH 2:13

This name of God appears in Jeremiah's prophecy in connection with the Lord's condemnation of the people of Judah for their idolatry. God found it hard to believe that they had rejected the waters of a flowing spring—or worship of the one true God. Instead they chose to drink stagnant water from a broken cistern—that is, to worship the pagan gods of surrounding nations that were untrustworthy and powerless.

This situation is not unique to Jeremiah's time. When we allow anything besides the Lord to take first place in our lives, it's like drinking contaminated water from a muddy pond. God wants only the best for us. He gives water in abundance from "the fountain of the water of life" to all who will come and drink (Revelation 21:6).

Jesus also used the imagery of refreshing water in His conversation with the woman at the well. He was the "living water" that could satisfy her spiritual thirst and bring meaning and purpose to her life (John 4:10).

Learn More: Psalm 36:9 / Jeremiah 17:13 / John 7:37–39 / Revelation 7:17

FREE SPIRIT

Restore unto me the joy of thy salvation;
and uphold me with thy free spirit.
Psalm 51:12

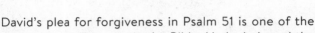

David's plea for forgiveness in Psalm 51 is one of the most eloquent prayers in the Bible. He had plotted the murder of Uriah, the husband of Bathsheba, to cover up his sin of adultery that had resulted in her pregnancy (2 Samuel 11:1–17). David's sin separated him from God. He prayed for the restoration of this relationship ("a right spirit," Psalm 51:10) through a movement of the Holy Spirit, which he described as God's "free spirit."

The Holy Spirit is free in the sense that He is not bound by our expectations. God is sovereign; He does not have to wait for our permission before He acts in His world. Sometimes His actions take us by surprise.

For example, it took a while for the early church to realize that the gospel was meant for all people, not just the Jews. The apostle Peter's famous vision, on the roof of Simon the tanner's house, convinced him that he "should not call any man common or unclean" (Acts 10:28). This insight came to Peter from the Holy Spirit, who brought many Gentiles to saving faith in Jesus Christ.

Learn More: John 16:13 / Acts 2:1–12

FRIEND OF PUBLICANS AND SINNERS

*The Son of man came eating and drinking,
and they say, Behold a man gluttonous, and a
winebibber, a friend of publicans and sinners.*
MATTHEW 11:19

The Pharisees criticized Jesus for associating with people whom they considered unworthy of God's love. But Jesus took their complaint as a compliment. He had been sent into the world to become the Savior of people like these.

In addition to befriending all sinners, Jesus was also a special friend to His disciples—the twelve ordinary men He trained to carry on the work after His earthly ministry came to an end. In Jesus' long farewell address in the Gospel of John, He told them, "Henceforth I call you not servants. . . but I have called you friends; for all things that I have heard of my Father I have made known unto you" (John 15:15).

Among the people whom we consider friends, one stands out above all others—our Lord Jesus Christ. He is the Friend who made the ultimate sacrifice on our behalf. "Greater love hath no man than this," He declared, "that a man lay down his life for his friends" (John 15:13).

Learn More: Mark 2:17 / Luke 5:30; 7:34; 15:1 / Romans 5:8 / 1 Timothy 1:15

FULLERS' SOAP

*But who may abide the day of his coming? and
who shall stand when he appeareth? for he is
like a refiner's fire, and like fullers' soap.*

MALACHI 3:2

This verse refers to the coming Messiah. The Jewish people
expected Him to be a conquering hero. But the prophet
Malachi declared that He would come in judgment against
the sinful nation of Israel.

A fuller made his living by washing and dyeing clothes or
the cloth used to make items to wear. Soap as we know it did
not exist in Bible times, so the fuller used a strong alkaline
substance to get the material clean. This cleaning agent
was made from a plant that was reduced to ashes to form
potash or lye. The imagery of a fuller is applied to Jesus'
dazzling clothes at His transfiguration. They were whiter
than any "fuller on earth [could] white them" (Mark 9:3).

The prophet Jeremiah pointed out that physical soap
was useless against the sins of the wayward people of Judah.
"For though thou wash thee with nitre, and take thee much
soap," he declared, "yet thine iniquity is marked before me,
saith the Lord GOD" (Jeremiah 2:22).

The name "fullers' soap" emphasizes the judgment
side of Jesus' ministry. He will return to earth in judgment
against those who refuse to accept Him as Lord and Savior
(2 Corinthians 5:10).

Learn More: Psalm 51:2, 7 / Isaiah 1:16; 7:3 / Mark 1:41

GIFT OF GOD

*If thou knewest the gift of God, and who
it is that saith to thee, Give me to drink;
thou wouldest have asked of him, and he
would have given thee living water.*

JOHN 4:10

Jesus spoke these words to the Samaritan woman at the
well (John 4:5–26). He made it clear that He was the "gift
of God" who had been sent into the world by the Father as
His agent of salvation.

A gift is something a person gives to others without
expecting anything in return. In spiritual terms, the element of grace should be added to this definition: God
through His Son gave us a gift that we could never earn
and certainly did not deserve.

Most of us have received gifts that we couldn't use or
that had to be returned because they were the wrong size
or color. But this is never so with God's gift of His Son. It
was selected with great care, it was given in love, and we
needed this gift more than anything in the world.

This familiar verse from the Gospel of John says it
all: "For God so loved the world, that he gave his only begotten Son, that whosoever believeth in him should not
perish, but have everlasting life" (John 3:16).

Learn More: Matthew 7:11 / Romans 6:23 /
2 Corinthians 9:15 / Ephesians 2:8

GLORY OF ISRAEL

For mine eyes have seen thy salvation. . .
a light to lighten the Gentiles, and the
glory of thy people Israel.
LUKE 2:30, 32

These verses are part of the prayer of Simeon when he recognized the infant Jesus as Messiah in the temple. Simeon realized that Jesus would grow up to become not only a light to the Gentiles but the glory of Israel as well.

As God's chosen people, the nation of Israel was commissioned to lead other nations to come to know Him as the one true God. Jesus was born into the world as a Jew and a native of Israel. In this sense, He was the glory of Israel, showing that God had not given up on His promise to bless the entire world through Abraham and his descendants (Genesis 12:1–3).

The tragedy is that Jesus was not accepted by many of His own people. They expected a Messiah who would restore Israel to its golden days as a political power. But God's purpose was not thwarted by their rejection. The glory of one nation, Israel, went on to become a light to the Gentiles, as Simeon predicted. At His return he will become the glorified One among all the peoples of the world (Philippians 2:11).

Learn More: Psalm 29:3 / Acts 7:2 / Colossians 1:27

GOD

*And Thomas answered and said
unto him, My Lord and my God.*
JOHN 20:28

This verse from the Gospel of John describes an appearance of Jesus to His disciples after the resurrection. Jesus had revealed Himself to them once before, at a time when Thomas was not present. Thomas had declared that he would not believe Jesus was alive unless he could see Him with his own eyes.

When Thomas finally saw the Lord, he not only believed the resurrection—he acknowledged Jesus as God in the flesh. This is one of the clearest statements in all the New Testament of the divinity of Jesus and His oneness with God the Father.

Thomas, like all the other disciples, had lived and worked with Jesus for about three years. They had seen His miracles and heard His teachings. They had observed firsthand that Jesus had the power and authority to forgive sin. But they were slow to understand that Jesus was actually God come to earth in human form.

As the God-man, Jesus is both the all-powerful deity for whom nothing is impossible and the man of sorrows who can sympathize with us in our human weakness. He is the all-sufficient Savior.

Learn More: Matthew 9:2 / John 1:1; 10:30; 14:9 /
1 Timothy 3:16

GOD OF ABRAHAM, ISAAC, AND JACOB

The LORD God of your fathers, the God of Abraham, the God of Isaac, and the God of Jacob, hath sent me unto you: this is my name for ever, and this is my memorial unto all generations.

EXODUS 3:15

God used this name for Himself when He called Moses to lead the Israelites out of slavery in Egypt. The Lord assured Moses that He had promised the land of Canaan to Abraham and his descendants many years before. God had not changed; He was the same God who would finally lead the Israelites to take the land and make it their own.

This promise had been renewed with Abraham's son Isaac, and then renewed again with Isaac's son Jacob. In Moses' time this promise had been all but forgotten. The Israelites had been in Egypt for more than four hundred years, suffering as slaves for part of that time (Exodus 12:40).

The message of this divine name is that God keeps His promises. Their fulfillment may take a while, but He will make good on what He is determined to do for His people.

Learn More: Exodus 3:6 / Matthew 22:32 / Acts 3:13

GOD OF ALL COMFORT

*Blessed be God, even the Father of
our Lord Jesus Christ, the Father of
mercies, and the God of all comfort.*
2 CORINTHIANS 1:3

The context of this verse makes it clear that the apostle Paul—when he spoke of the Lord as the "God of all comfort"—was thinking of the sufferings that believers endure. We as Christians are often ridiculed by the world for our beliefs and the stands we take. But our persecution should not lead us to despair. God's comforting presence enables us to remain joyful and optimistic in spite of our pain (James 1:2).

Jesus described the Holy Spirit as a Comforter who would strengthen the disciples after He was no longer with them in the flesh (John 14:16–26). "And I will pray the Father, and he shall give you another Comforter," Jesus promised, "that he may abide with you for ever" (John 14:16).

Because we know and feel God's presence, we are expected to serve as agents of God's comfort in the lives of others. The apostle Paul declared that we should "comfort them which are in any trouble, by the comfort wherewith we ourselves are comforted of God" (2 Corinthians 1:4).

Learn More: Psalm 23:4; 119:76 / Isaiah 12:1; 49:13; 61:2 / Zechariah 1:17

GOD OF GODS

The king answered unto Daniel, and said,
Of a truth it is, that your God is a God of gods,
and a Lord of kings, and a revealer of secrets,
seeing thou couldest reveal this secret.
DANIEL 2:47

King Nebuchadnezzar of Babylon had a disturbing dream about a huge statue. None of his pagan wizards could interpret the dream. But the prophet Daniel told the king what the dream meant after declaring that it would be revealed to him by the one true God.

This pagan king was so impressed by this interpretation of his dream that he declared Daniel's God to be the "God of gods"—or the God above all the other deities in the kingdom of Babylon. This was a shocking admission, since the Babylonians had a god for every need and purpose—war, fertility, science, literature, and so on. This type of worship—known as polytheism, or belief in many deities—was typical of all the pagan nations during Bible times.

As Christians, we know that the one true God is capable of mighty acts. But like King Nebuchadnezzar, sometimes even we are overwhelmed with His awesome deeds.

Two other divine names that express the superiority of the Lord to all false gods are "King of kings" and "Lord of lords" (Revelation 17:14).

Learn More: Joshua 22:22 / Psalm 136:2 / Daniel 11:36

*And it came to pass, when I heard
these words, that I sat down and wept,
and mourned certain days, and fasted,
and prayed before the God of heaven.*

NEHEMIAH 1:4

This verse describes Nehemiah's reaction when he heard disturbing news about the Jewish exiles who had gone back to their homeland. The Persian king had allowed them to return to rebuild the city of Jerusalem. But the work was at a standstill, and the Jews were being persecuted by their enemies.

Nehemiah's name for God in this verse appears multiple times in his book (Nehemiah 1:5; 2:4, 20) as well as the book of Ezra (Ezra 5:12; 6:9–10; 7:21, 23). These two books describe the bleak conditions of God's people after the exile. They had lived for several decades as captives of the pagan nations of Babylon and Persia. They had to start life all over again when they were finally allowed to return to their homeland.

Perhaps the Israelites had a hard time seeing God at work among them during these turbulent times. But Ezra and Nehemiah assured them that God was still in His heaven and had not forsaken His people. We as believers have this same assurance.

Learn More: Genesis 24:3 / 2 Chronicles 36:23 / Psalm 136:26 / Jonah 1:9

GOD OF MY SALVATION

Although the fig tree shall not blossom, neither shall fruit be in the vines; the labour of the olive shall fail, and the fields shall yield no meat; the flock shall be cut off from the fold, and there shall be no herd in the stalls: Yet I will rejoice in the LORD, I will joy in the God of my salvation.

HABAKKUK 3:17–18

This passage from the little-known prophet Habakkuk is one of the most beautiful in the Bible. It is filled with agricultural imagery from the prophet's time, including crop failures and the loss of livestock. But Habakkuk's faith allowed him to see beyond the troubles of the moment to the deeper reality that the God of his salvation was in charge. He would not let the prophet down.

Rephrased in modern terms, Habakkuk's sentiments might read something like this: "Although the grocery money is gone, energy prices are going through the ceiling, our mortgage payment just jumped by four hundred dollars a month, and I don't know where the next meal is coming from, I will rejoice in the Lord and continue to trust in the God of my salvation."

Learn More: Exodus 15:2 / Job 13:16 / Micah 7:7

GOD OF PEACE

*Now the God of peace, that brought again
from the dead our Lord Jesus. . .through the
blood of the everlasting covenant, make you
perfect in every good work to do his will,
working in you that which is wellpleasing in
his sight, through Jesus Christ; to whom
be glory for ever and ever. Amen.*

HEBREWS 13:20–21

The author of the epistle to the Hebrews brought his book to a close with a request for the blessings of "the God of peace" to rest upon His people. This is one of the most beautiful benedictions in the Bible.

Some people think of peace as the absence of conflict. But peace, according to the New Testament, is the inner tranquility of those who have placed their trust in Jesus Christ and have been reconciled to God because their sins have been forgiven.

The Lord is the God of peace because He sent His own Son to allow us to experience this sense of well-being. This is how the apostle Paul expressed it: "Therefore being justified by faith, we have peace with God through our Lord Jesus Christ" (Romans 5:1).

Learn More: Romans 15:33; 16:20 / Philippians 4:9

GOD OF THE
WHOLE EARTH

For thy Maker is thine husband; the LORD *of
hosts is his name; and thy Redeemer the Holy
One of Israel; The God of the whole earth shall
he be called.*
ISAIAH 54:5

This name of God from the prophet Isaiah emphasizes the Lord's unlimited jurisdiction. There is no place on earth where His authority is limited. This idea is the opposite of the view of most pagan nations of Bible times, which believed their gods were local or regional in scope. These deities existed to serve certain people's needs and protect them from their enemies, so their authority as gods did not extend beyond national borders.

This is why the Syrian military commander Naaman, after he was healed by the prophet Elisha in Israelite territory, wanted to carry dirt from Israel back to his own country (2 Kings 5:17). Naaman thought this miracle-working God was a regional deity whose power he could transfer to his own people.

The Lord's presence doesn't have to be carried back and forth from one country to another. He already exists in every place, as the supreme God over all the world. The psalmist declared, "The earth is the LORD's, and the fulness thereof; the world, and they that dwell therein" (Psalm 24:1).

Learn More: Genesis 14:19; 18:25 / Joshua 3:13 /
Psalm 47:2 / Micah 4:3

GOD WHO SEES

*And she [Hagar] called the name of the
LORD that spake unto her, Thou God
seest me: for she said, Have I also here
looked after him that seeth me?*
GENESIS 16:13

Sarah's servant, Hagar, called God by this name when the
angel of the Lord appeared to her in the wilderness. After
conceiving a child by Abraham, Hagar had been driven
away by Sarah, Abraham's wife. The Lord assured Hagar
that He was aware of her plight, and He would bless her
and others through the life of her unborn child.

After Hagar gave birth, she named the boy Ishmael,
meaning "God hears." Her experience shows that the
Lord is not a distant and detached God who refuses to get
involved in our lives. He sees our needs, hears our prayers,
and comes to our aid in times of trouble.

The Bible speaks often of the Lord as the all-seeing One
who knows what is going on in His world and who keeps
watch over His people. The psalmist declared, "The eyes
of the LORD are upon the righteous, and his ears are open
unto their cry" (Psalm 34:15).

Learn More: 2 Chronicles 16:9 / Proverbs 15:3 /
Jeremiah 7:11 / Amos 9:8 / 1 Peter 3:12

GOOD MASTER

There came one running, and kneeled to him,
and asked him, Good Master, what shall I
do that I may inherit eternal life?
MARK 10:17

This account of Jesus' encounter with a man seeking eternal life appears in the three Synoptic Gospels: Matthew tells us he was young (Matthew 19:22); Mark reveals that he was rich (Mark 10:22); Luke adds that he was a ruler (Luke 18:18). Thus, he is known as the "rich young ruler."

This young man called Jesus "Good Master" and bowed before Him. He respected Jesus and recognized Him as a teacher of authority. But Jesus corrected him for calling Him "good." "There is none good but one," He replied, "that is, God" (Mark 10:18).

Why did Jesus resist this name? Perhaps He saw "good" as meaningless flattery. Or this may have been His way of testing the young man's commitment to God the Father, who held the keys to eternal life—the very thing he was seeking. The rich young ruler wanted to know what he could *do* to have eternal life. Jesus made it clear that this is a gift that God bestows on those who follow His commands.

This young man was more committed to his riches than he was to following the Lord. Tragically, this kept him from finding what he was searching for.

Learn More: Matthew 8:19 / Mark 9:5 / Luke 8:24

GOOD SHEPHERD

*I am the good shepherd: the good shepherd
giveth his life for the sheep.*
JOHN 10:11

This verse is part of a long monologue of Jesus in which He compares His followers to sheep and identifies Himself as the Shepherd who leads His flock (John 10:1–16).

In the Old Testament, God is also known by the name "shepherd" (Psalm 23:1). Sheep were helpless animals that had no natural defenses against predators such as wolves and lions. Unless they were watched constantly, sheep would wander away from the flock and find themselves in danger. They had to be led from one area to another to find new sources of food and water. Sheep needed a vigilant leader—a shepherd—to provide all these resources.

But Jesus is more than just another shepherd. He is the "*good* shepherd." He deliberately set Himself apart from the religious leaders of Israel—the scribes and Pharisees—who were leading people astray. They were like "hirelings" (John 10:12), hired hands who were paid to do a job but had no personal interest in the sheep they were leading. Jesus loved His sheep—that includes you and me—and He eventually gave His life for our salvation.

Learn More: John 10:7 / Hebrews 13:20 / 1 Peter 2:25; 5:4

GOOD SPIRIT

Thou gavest also thy good spirit to instruct them, and withheldest not thy manna from their mouth, and gavest them water for their thirst.
NEHEMIAH 9:20

This verse describes the provision of God for the Israelites in the wilderness after their release from slavery in Egypt. These words were spoken in Nehemiah's time by Levites who led the people to renew the covenant with God the Father. They described the Holy Spirit as God's "good spirit."

Because the very essence of God is goodness, He showered His people with goodness during the perilous years of wandering in the wilderness. He led them by His presence in a cloud and fire, encouraged them with His promise of a land of their own, and gave them instructions for life in the laws He delivered to Moses. Through His "good spirit," God provided many good things for His people.

The Lord is still the God of goodness who provides abundantly for believers through His Spirit. He expects us to exemplify this spirit of goodness to others. The apostle Paul told the believers at Rome that he was "persuaded of you, my brethren, that ye also are full of goodness, filled with all knowledge, able also to admonish one another" (Romans 15:14).

Learn More: John 16:13 / Romans 8:11 / Galatians 5:22

GOVERNOR

And thou Bethlehem, in the land of Juda,
art not the least among the princes of Juda:
for out of thee shall come a Governor,
that shall rule my people Israel.

MATTHEW 2:6

The world into which Jesus was born knew all about governors, or rulers. These officials were agents set over the provinces—territories similar to states—into which the Roman government had divided its empire. A provincial governor was responsible for collecting taxes for the Roman treasury, keeping the peace, and administering the rule of Rome. Three Roman governors are mentioned in the New Testament: Cyrenius (Luke 2:2), Pontius Pilate (Matthew 27:2), and Felix (Acts 23:24).

But Jesus is a Governor of a different type. He was sent as a spiritual ruler to guide and direct His people in the ways of the Lord. He rules by love and not by force. As believers, our lives should reflect more of His rule every day as we grow in our commitment to Him and His teachings.

Governors of states and nations come and go, but Jesus' rule over His followers is eternal. As the prophet Isaiah declared, "Of the increase of his government and peace there shall be no end" (Isaiah 9:7).

Learn More: Isaiah 40:10; 55:4 / Micah 5:2

GREAT HIGH PRIEST

Seeing then that we have a great high priest,
that is passed into the heavens, Jesus the Son
of God, let us hold fast our profession.
HEBREWS 4:14

Priests of the Bible offered various types of sacrifices on behalf of the people to atone for their sins. This name of Jesus from the book of Hebrews reflects this priestly imagery of the Jewish religious system.

At the top of the priestly hierarchy stood the high priest. His job was to see that all the functions of the priesthood were carried out appropriately (2 Chronicles 19:11). Below him were other priests who performed sacrificial rituals at the altar. On the lower end of the priesthood were the Levites, who performed menial jobs as assistants to the priests.

The writer of Hebrews adds another level to this priestly hierarchy by referring to Jesus as the "great high priest." He stands above even the high priest of Israel because He laid down His own life as the perfect sacrifice for sin.

In modern terms, a priest is a religious leader who intercedes between God and man on behalf of sinful people. As believers, we need no human intermediary to represent us before God. We can come directly into His presence through "one mediator between God and men, the man Christ Jesus" (1 Timothy 2:5). See also *High Priest after the Order of Melchisedec*.

Learn More: Hebrews 2:17; 3:1; 6:20; 7:17

GREAT PROPHET

And there came a fear on all: and they glorified God, saying, That a great prophet is risen up among us; and, That God hath visited his people.

LUKE 7:16

This verse describes the reaction of the people of Nain when Jesus raised the son of a widow from the dead. Perhaps they were comparing Jesus to Elijah, the famous prophet of Old Testament times, who also brought back from the dead the son of a poor widow (1 Kings 17:17–24).

The classic definition of a prophet in the Jewish tradition is that he should declare God's message to the people and he should foretell the future. Jesus fit this definition perfectly. He was the ultimate Prophet in a long line of prophets whom God had sent to His people, the Israelites, across many centuries.

A true prophet must be committed to declaring God's truth, no matter how his message is received. He accepts the fact that he will never be the most popular person in town. It was no different with Jesus. Some of the saddest words He ever uttered were spoken after He was rejected by the people of His own hometown: "A prophet is not without honour, save in his own country, and in his own house" (Matthew 13:57).

Learn More: Matthew 21:11 / Luke 24:19 / John 6:14

GUIDE UNTO DEATH

For this God is our God for ever and ever:
he will be our guide even unto death.
PSALM 48:14

The unknown author of this psalm made the same declaration that King David did when he wrote the Twenty-third Psalm. God will abide with us and continue to lead us, even through the experience of death itself. As David expressed it, "Yea, though I walk through the valley of the shadow of death, I will fear no evil: for thou art with me" (Psalm 23:4).

A guide is a person who can lead us safely on a trip or an adventure because he knows the best path to follow. He can help us avoid any obstacles on the way to our destination. With the Lord as our guide, we don't have to fear death. He will take us to dwell in glory with Him when our days on earth come to an end.

The prophet Jeremiah spoke of God as "the guide of my youth" (Jeremiah 3:4). It is comforting to know that whether our life is just beginning or coming to an end, we can trust God as our never-failing guide.

Learn More: Job 30:23 / Psalm 119:105 / Romans 8:38–39 / 1 Corinthians 15:55 / Revelation 21:4

HEAD OF ALL PRINCIPALITY AND POWER

*For in him dwelleth all the fulness of the
Godhead bodily. And ye are complete in him,
which is the head of all principality and power.*
COLOSSIANS 2:9–10

In this verse the apostle Paul dealt with a false teaching in
the church at Colossae. Some members of this congregation were claiming that Jesus was a member of an order
of angels, thus a created being like all other things made
by God. Paul declared that Jesus was actually the "head
of all principality and power," or a noncreated being who
was above all heavenly beings, with the exception of God
Himself. And even in His relationship to God, Jesus reflected
"all the fulness of the Godhead."

Just as Jesus is supreme in the heavens, He also exercises
dominion over all the earth. As the apostle Paul expressed
it, "For by him were all things created, that are in heaven,
and that are in earth, visible and invisible, whether they be
thrones, or dominions, or principalities, or powers: all things
were created by him, and for him" (Colossians 1:16). This
truth should drive us to our knees in worship and praise.

Learn More: Ephesians 1:21–22 / Revelation 17:14

HEAD OF THE CHURCH

For the husband is the head of the wife,
even as Christ is the head of the church:
and he is the saviour of the body.

EPHESIANS 5:23

The word *disciple* means "learner"—and that's exactly what Jesus' disciples were. They learned from Jesus—who He was, about the mission on which He had been sent, and of God's love for all people. Jesus trained these ordinary men to carry on His work through the church He brought into being.

On one occasion Jesus told Peter, "Upon this rock I will build my church" (Matthew 16:18). Peter had just declared his belief that Jesus was the long-awaited Messiah and "the Son of the living God" (Matthew 16:16). Jesus was saying that His church would be built on confessions of faith just like the one Peter had made. The church would consist of people who accepted Jesus as Savior and Lord and committed themselves to His work of redemption in the world.

Jesus is the "head of the church," and we as believers make up the body. A body without a head is useless, but a body joined to a head becomes a living, breathing, working organism. The church is still the key element in Jesus' strategy to bring the world into God's kingdom.

Learn More: Ephesians 1:22; 5:24 / Colossians 1:18

HEAD OF THE CORNER

Jesus saith unto them, Did ye never read in the scriptures, The stone which the builders rejected, the same is become the head of the corner: this is the Lord's doing, and it is marvellous in our eyes?
MATTHEW 21:42

Jesus directed these words to the religious leaders who were questioning His authority. He quoted Psalm 118:22–23, an Old Testament passage that they probably knew well. His point was that He, as the Messiah, was destined to be rejected by them.

But Jesus, the rejected stone, would become the centerpiece of a new building that would include all people who accepted Him as Savior and Lord. This building would be the church, a fresh, new organism that would be born out of the ashes of the old religious order based on the Jewish law.

The apostle Peter also referenced this same verse from the Psalms (1 Peter 2:7). Peter went on to say that Jesus, the rejected stone, was also "a stone of stumbling, and a rock of offence" (1 Peter 2:8) to those people who thought the Messiah would be a political and military leader. It was unthinkable to them that He would come as a spiritual deliverer who would suffer and die on the cross.

Learn More: Isaiah 28:16 / Mark 12:10 / Luke 20:17 / Acts 4:11 / Ephesians 2:19–20

HEIR OF ALL THINGS

God, who. . .spake in time past unto the
fathers by the prophets, hath in these last
days spoken unto us by his Son, whom
he hath appointed heir of all things.
HEBREWS 1:1–2

The dictionary defines an heir as "one who receives some endowment or quality from a parent or predecessor." Many heirs receive only a portion of the property or cash that their parents have accumulated during a lifetime. But the writer of Hebrews declared that Jesus was the "heir of all things," and these were granted to Him by none other than God the Father.

The heirship of Jesus is both material and spiritual. He participated with God in the creation of the world (John 1:3), so God has granted Jesus dominion over the universe. In the spiritual sense, He sets the terms by which all people will be judged for their sins. Then He Himself became the means by which people could be made righteous in God's sight. This was accomplished through His death on the cross.

The great thing about Jesus' spiritual heirship is that He shares His inheritance with us. As the apostle Paul expressed it, we are "joint-heirs with Christ" (Romans 8:17) because He lives eternally with the Father and He has made it possible for us to enjoy eternal life with Him.

Learn More: Galatians 3:29; 4:7 / Titus 3:7 / James 2:5

HIDING PLACE

*Thou art my hiding place; thou shalt preserve
me from trouble; thou shalt compass me
about with songs of deliverance.*

PSALM 32:7

This name of God appears in a psalm attributed to David, king of Israel. During his early years, he had to flee for his life because the jealous King Saul was trying to kill him. Once David hid in a cave, and he later wrote about this experience in one of his psalms (1 Samuel 22:1; Psalm 142 title).

The problem with a physical hiding place is that it can't last forever. David eventually had to come out of his cave for food and water. But he found the Lord to be his ultimate "hiding place." He kept David safe until Saul was killed in a battle with the Philistines and David became the unchallenged king of the nation of Israel.

There's no safer place for any of us to be than under the protective hand of a loving, benevolent God. As the psalmist expressed it, "I will both lay me down in peace, and sleep: for thou, LORD, only makest me dwell in safety" (Psalm 4:8).

Learn More: Psalm 17:8; 27:5; 143:9 / Proverbs 29:25

He [Jesus] became the author of eternal salvation. . .called of God an high priest after the order of Melchisedec.
HEBREWS 5:9–10

This name refers to one of the most mysterious personalities of the Bible. Melchisedec was the king of Salem—an ancient name for Jerusalem—and a priest of the Most High God. He appeared to Abraham after the patriarch had defeated several kings who had carried his nephew Lot away as a captive.

When Abraham returned from battle with the spoils of war, Melchisedec blessed him and provided food for him and his hungry men. In return, Abraham presented Melchisedec with a tithe—one-tenth of the booty they had taken (Genesis 14:12–20).

The author of Hebrews called Jesus a "high priest after the Order of Melchisedec" because Melchisedec did not become a priest by virtue of his birth. He was not a descendant of Aaron, the first high priest of Israel through whose family line all succeeding priests of Israel emerged.

Just like Melchisedec, Jesus did not inherit His priestly responsibilities. He was appointed to this role by God the Father. His priesthood has no beginning or end, so it is superior to the inherited priesthood and the sacrificial system of the Old Testament (Hebrews 7:23–24). See also *Great High Priest.*

Learn More: Hebrews 2:17; 3:1; 6:20; 7:17

HOLY ONE

I am the LORD, your Holy One,
the creator of Israel, your King.
ISAIAH 43:15

This divine name is one of the few in the Bible that is applied to all three persons of the Trinity—Father (Isaiah 43:15), Son (Acts 3:14), and Holy Spirit (1 John 2:20). Holiness expresses the idea of separation. The Lord exists on a different level than all earthly things—He is perfect in His moral excellence, unlike sinful people.

The apostle Peter called Jesus "the Holy One" to contrast the righteousness of Jesus with the unrighteousness of Barabbas, a criminal whom the crowd released instead of Jesus on the day of His crucifixion (Acts 3:14). Jesus is also the Holy One because He resisted sin through His close relationship with God the Father.

The apostle John declared that one role of the Holy Spirit as the Holy One was to keep believers from erroneous thinking about the nature of Jesus. Some false teachers in John's time were claiming that Jesus was the divine Son of God but denying that He had come to earth in human form. The Holy Spirit filled believers with the truth about Jesus (1 John 2:20).

We as believers will never achieve complete holiness in this life. We will always struggle with temptation and our sinful nature. But we ought to be growing more and more like Jesus in this dimension of the Christian life.

Learn More: Isaiah 12:6; 29:23; 60:9

*Let no corrupt communication proceed out
of your mouth, but that which is good. . .that
it may minister grace unto the hearers. And
grieve not the holy Spirit of God, whereby ye
are sealed unto the day of redemption.*
EPHESIANS 4:29–30

These words from the apostle Paul to the believers at Ephesus emphasize several important truths about the Holy Spirit.

The Holy Spirit can be grieved or pained by the sinful actions of believers. This shows that the Holy Spirit is not a vague force but a person. Only a person can experience emotions like grief and sorrow; thus, the Spirit is not an "it" but a "He." He is as much a person as God the Father and Jesus the Son.

This verse also emphasizes the "sealing" work of the Holy Spirit. A seal symbolizes ownership and security. The seal of the Holy Spirit marks believers as God's property until the day of our final redemption in the end time (Romans 8:23).

If some actions by believers grieve the Holy Spirit, it follows that certain acts and attitudes bring Him joy and pleasure. These include the fruits of the Spirit in the apostle Paul's famous list in Galatians 5:22–23.

Learn More: Psalm 51:11 / Luke 11:13 / John 14:26 /
1 Thessalonians 4:8

HOPE OF GLORY

To whom God would make known
what is the riches of the glory of this
mystery among the Gentiles; which is
Christ in you, the hope of glory.
COLOSSIANS 1:27

The apostle Paul is known as the "apostle to the Gentiles," but he could also be called the "apostle of hope." His writings abound with the theme of the hope that believers have in the promises of Jesus Christ.

In this verse from his letter to the Colossian believers, Paul called Jesus the "hope of glory." If we know Christ as our Savior and Lord, we are assured that we will live with Him in His full glory when we reach our heavenly home.

The writer of Hebrews described our hope in Jesus as an "anchor of the soul" (Hebrews 6:19). He is the great stabilizing force that helps us live victoriously in spite of the difficulties and problems of life.

To hope in something is to look forward to its fulfillment with confident expectation. Notice that Paul said in this verse that "Christ in you" is our hope of glory. With Jesus as a constant presence in our lives, we are as certain of heaven as if we were already there.

Learn More: Romans 15:13 / Colossians 1:23 / Titus 3:7

HORN OF MY SALVATION

The LORD is my rock, and my fortress,
and my deliverer; my God, my strength,
in whom I will trust; my buckler, and the
horn of my salvation, and my high tower.

PSALM 18:2

David wrote this psalm to express his praise to God for saving him from "all his enemies, and from the hand of Saul" (Psalm 18 title). In Bible times the horn of an animal was a symbol of strength. To lift one's horn in arrogance like an ox was to show pride and power (Psalm 75:4–5). Thus, God had been a "horn of salvation" on David's behalf by delivering him from those who were trying to kill him.

This imagery from the Old Testament was picked up in the New Testament and applied to Jesus in a spiritual sense. Zacharias, the father of John the Baptist, declared that God through His Son had "raised up an horn of salvation for us in the house of his servant David" (Luke 1:69).

This verse is part of the song of praise known as the "Benedictus" that Zacharias sang at the birth of his son John, the forerunner of Jesus (Luke 1:67–79). Zacharias stated that Jesus was the king of salvation from the kingly line of David. The horn imagery as applied to Jesus declared that He would be a powerful Savior.

Learn More: Exodus 15:2 / 2 Samuel 22:3 / Job 13:16 / Micah 7:7

HUSBAND

*I will make a new covenant with the house
of Israel, and with the house of Judah: Not
according to the covenant that I made with their
fathers in the day that I took them by the hand
to bring them out of the land of Egypt; which
my covenant they brake, although I was an
husband unto them, saith the LORD.*
JEREMIAH 31:31–32

This name of God appears in the prophet Jeremiah's description of the new covenant that God will make with His people. The Lord had led the Israelites out of Egypt and through the wilderness like a loving husband takes care of his wife. But He would provide even more abundantly for His people by sending the Messiah, who would save them from their sins.

The imagery of God as a husband appears in only one other place in the Bible. The prophet Isaiah told the people of Israel: "Thy Maker is thine husband; the LORD of hosts is his name" (Isaiah 54:5).

The role of a husband involves more than providing for the physical needs of his family. He should also be an encourager, a listener, an emotional support, and a protector for his wife and children. God as a loving husband provides all of these things in abundance for His people.

Learn More: 2 Corinthians 11:2 / Revelation 21:2

I AM

Jesus said unto them, Verily, verily, I say unto
you, Before Abraham was, I am. Then took they
up stones to cast at him: but Jesus hid himself,
and went out of the temple, going through the
midst of them, and so passed by.
JOHN 8:58–59

This name that Jesus called Himself is the equivalent of the name with which God identified Himself to Moses at the burning bush. Just like the great "I Am" of the Old Testament, Jesus was claiming to be eternal, timeless, and unchanging. He had always been and He would always be. In other words, He was of the same divine essence as God the Father.

This claim of divinity was blasphemy to the Jewish religious leaders, so they picked up stones to execute Him—the penalty for such a crime spelled out in the Old Testament law (Leviticus 24:16). But Jesus' escape proved the claim He was making. He easily avoided their death threat as He slipped miraculously "through the midst of them." Only when the time was right in accordance with God's plan would He allow Himself to be captured and crucified.

Other "I Am" statements of Jesus appear throughout John's Gospel (see Learn More passages below).

Learn More: John 6:35; 8:12; 10:7, 11, 36; 11:25; 14:6; 15:1

I AM THAT I AM

And God said unto Moses, I Aᴍ Tʜᴀᴛ I Aᴍ:
and he said, Thus shalt thou say unto the
children of Israel, I Aᴍ hath sent me unto you.
Exodus 3:14

When God appeared in the burning bush, Moses wanted to know who was sending him back to Egypt to lead the Israelites out of slavery. Moses may have been puzzled by the Lord's reply that "I Am That I Am" was behind this plan.

This name for God is a form of the verb "to be" in the Hebrew language. It expresses God's self-existence and the unchangeable nature of His character. He transcends the past, the present, and the future. We might express the meaning of this name like this: He has always been in the past, He is in the present, and He will always be in the future.

This is the only place in the Bible where this name appears. But Jehovah or Yahweh, generally rendered as "Lord," is a closely related name that also comes from the Hebrew form of "to be." This name appears hundreds of times throughout the Old Testament. In most translations of the Bible, it appears with a large capital "L" and smaller capital letters like this: Lᴏʀᴅ.

Learn More: Deuteronomy 33:27 / Psalm 90:2 / 1 Timothy 1:17

IMMANUEL / EMMANUEL

*Behold, a virgin shall conceive, and bear a son,
and shall call his name Immanuel.*
ISAIAH 7:14

This prophecy from Isaiah was fulfilled with the birth of Jesus (Matthew 1:22–23). The name, meaning "God with us," was given to Jesus even before He was born by an angel who appeared to Joseph. He needed divine assurance that Mary's pregnancy was an act of the Holy Spirit and that he should proceed to take her as his wife.

The promise of God's presence among His people goes back to Old Testament times. For example, He assured Moses of His presence (Exodus 3:12) when giving him the task to free the Israelites from their slavery in Egypt. King David declared that God's presence would follow him wherever he went (Psalm 139:9–10).

These promises reach their peak in God's Son, Jesus Christ. He came to earth in the form of the God-man to show that God is for us in our weak, sinful, and helpless condition. As man, He understands our temptations and shortcomings. As God, He can meet all these needs through His love and grace.

Just as Matthew's Gospel begins with the affirmation that God is with us, so it ends with Jesus' promise of His abiding presence: "Lo, I am with you always, even unto the end of the world" (Matthew 28:20).

Learn More: Exodus 33:14 / Psalm 139:7 / John 14:18 / Romans 8:35 / Hebrews 13:5

JEHOVAH

*And I appeared unto Abraham, unto Isaac, and
unto Jacob, by the name of God Almighty, but
by my name JEHOVAH was I not known to them.*
EXODUS 6:3

With these words the Lord reassured Moses that He would
stand with him and give him the strength and power to lead
the Israelites out of Egyptian slavery. He had already given
Moses this promise at the burning bush (Exodus 3:2, 12).
But Moses needed encouragement after Pharaoh rejected
his first request to release the Israelites.

God declared to Moses that He was prepared to perform
miracles for His people, things they had never seen before.
As Jehovah, He was the infinite and self-existent God who
caused everything to happen and to whom all things must
eventually be traced. He would not fail in His determination
to bring freedom to His people.

In his messages to the wayward people of Judah, the
prophet Isaiah declared, "Trust ye in the LORD for ever: for
in the Lord Jehovah is everlasting strength (Isaiah 26:4).

Learn More: Psalm 83:18 / Isaiah 12:2

JEHOVAH-JIREH

And Abraham called the name of that place Jehovahjireh: as it is said to this day, In the mount of the LORD it shall be seen.
GENESIS 22:14

Abraham called God by this name and assigned it to the site where he was told to sacrifice his son, Isaac, as a burnt offering to the Lord. This was God's way of testing Abraham's faith and obedience.

When Abraham raised a knife to take Isaac's life, God stopped him. Then Abraham noticed a ram that had been trapped in a nearby thicket. He offered this ram as a sacrifice instead of Isaac. It was clear to him that God had provided a sacrificial animal for this purpose—thus the name *Jehovahjireh*, or "The Lord Will Provide" as rendered by modern translations.

God still delights in providing for His people. Jesus assured us of this in His sermon on the mount. "Behold the fowls of the air," He declared, "for they sow not, neither do they reap, nor gather into barns; yet your heavenly Father feedeth them. Are ye not much better than they" (Matthew 6:26).

Learn More: Psalm 37:4 / Matthew 6:8 / Philippians 4:19

JEHOVAH-NISSI

*And Moses built an altar, and called
the name of it Jehovahnissi.*
EXODUS 17:15

Moses gave this name to an altar that he built in the wilderness near Rephidim. The altar memorialized an Israelite victory over the Amalekites because of God's miraculous intervention on their behalf. Most modern translations render these two Hebrew words as "The LORD Is My Banner."

In Bible times, armies fought under a banner or battle flag that identified their tribe or nation. "Jehovah-nissi" was Moses' way of saying that the Israelites in the wilderness did not need such a flag. The Lord was the banner under which they fought, and He had given the victory.

When the Israelites entered the land of Canaan, the Lord gave them many victories, beginning with the capture of Jericho. They conquered this fortified city without firing a single arrow because the Lord caused the defensive walls to collapse (Joshua 6:20).

In a messianic passage in his book, the prophet Isaiah looked forward to the coming of the Messiah, whom he described as an "ensign," or battle flag (Isaiah 11:10).

Learn More: Psalm 20:5 / Song of Solomon 2:4 / Isaiah 5:26

JEHOVAH-SHALOM

And the L<small>ORD</small> said unto him, Peace be
unto thee; fear not: thou shalt not die.
Then Gideon built an altar there unto
the L<small>ORD</small>, and called it Jehovahshalom.
J<small>UDGES</small> 6:23–24

Gideon was given the task of delivering God's people from Midianite raiders who were destroying their crops and stealing their livestock. The Lord assured Gideon of His presence and guidance by burning up a sacrificial offering that Gideon placed on an altar.

This display frightened Gideon. But God showed that His intentions were peaceful and that Gideon had nothing to fear. With this assurance, Gideon gave God a special name, *Jehovahshalom*—translated as "The Lord Is Peace" by modern translations—and also applied this name to the altar he had built.

"Peace to you and your house" was a common greeting of Bible times, just as we greet people today with "Good morning" or "How are you?" With this divine name, Gideon expressed his confidence that God intended to bless him and to strengthen him for the task to which he had been called.

God extends this same promise to His people today. The psalmist declared, "The L<small>ORD</small> will give strength unto his people; the L<small>ORD</small> will bless his people with peace" (Psalm 29:11).

Learn More: Isaiah 9:6 / Romans 15:33 / Hebrews 13:20

JESUS

*And when eight days were accomplished for
the circumcising of the child, his name was
called JESUS, which was so named of the angel
before he was conceived in the womb.*

LUKE 2:21

Jewish custom dictated that a male child be circumcised
and named on the eighth day after he was born. Mary and
Joseph followed this custom with Jesus. They had been
told by an angel even before the birth that His name would
be Jesus. They followed the angel's instruction by giving
Him this name.

The name *Jesus* is the equivalent of the Old Testament
name rendered variously as Jehoshua (Numbers 13:16),
Jeshua (Ezra 2:2), and Joshua (Exodus 17:9). It means
"Jehovah (or Yahweh) Is Salvation." Thus Jesus' personal
name indicated from the very beginning that He was to be
God's agent of salvation in a dark and sinful world.

When the Lord was born, *Jesus* was actually a common
name among the Jewish people, similar to "John" or "Robert"
in our society. But His life and ministry have made the
name a synonym for self-giving love. In the words of the
apostle Paul, it is the "name which is above every name"
(Philippians 2:9).

Learn More: Matthew 1:21, 25 / Luke 1:31

JUDGE OF ALL THE EARTH

That be far from thee to do after this manner,
to slay the righteous with the wicked. . . .
Shall not the Judge of all the earth do right?
GENESIS 18:25

Abraham called the Lord by this name when they discussed God's decision to destroy the city of Sodom. The residents of this city, along with Gomorrah, had grown so wicked that God was determined to wipe them from the face of the earth. Abraham believed that God was just in all His actions. Surely "the Judge of all the earth" would not destroy the righteous people of Sodom along with the wicked.

God did follow through on His plan to destroy the city. But He sent an angel to warn the only righteous people in Sodom—Lot and his family—to flee before the judgment fell (Genesis 19:1, 15–17). This proved that the Lord is fair and equitable in His dispensing of justice in this world. The psalmist declared, "Justice and judgment are the habitation of thy throne: mercy and truth shall go before thy face" (Psalm 89:14).

Learn More: 1 Chronicles 16:33 / Psalm 94:2 / Hebrews 12:23

JUDGE OF QUICK AND DEAD

And he commanded us to preach unto the people,
and to testify that it is he which was ordained
of God to be the Judge of quick and dead.
ACTS 10:42

This name of Jesus appears in a sermon that the apostle Peter preached to the Roman centurion Cornelius (Acts 10:25–43). Peter declared that Jesus had been appointed by God the Father as the supreme Judge of all things—the living ("quick") and the dead.

God's activity as Judge is one of the key themes of the Old Testament. But after God sent Jesus into the world, He established a new way of rendering judgment. Jesus is now the agent through whom divine judgment is handed down (John 5:22).

As the divine Judge, Jesus is the great dividing line in history. At the "great white throne" judgment in the end times, those who have refused to accept Him as Savior and Lord will be consigned to eternal separation from God (Revelation 20:11–15). Believers will escape this judgment because they have accepted the sacrifice that Jesus has made on their behalf.

Christians will be subjected to an evaluation known as the "judgment seat of Christ." The service they have rendered for Jesus Christ will be judged and rewarded accordingly. This principle of accountability should motivate us to loyal service in His name.

Learn More: Romans 4:17; 6:11; 8:11 / 2 Timothy 4:8

JUST MAN

When he [Pilate] was set down on the judgment seat, his wife sent unto him, saying, Have thou nothing to do with that just man: for I have suffered many things this day in a dream because of him.

MATTHEW 27:19

Pontius Pilate, the Roman governor who condemned Jesus to death, received this message from his wife while Jesus was on trial. It had been revealed to her in a dream that Jesus was innocent of the charges against Him, so she tried to get Pilate to release Him.

Pilate also knew that Jesus was not guilty, but he caved in to political pressure from the Jewish religious leaders and pronounced the death penalty against Him. The governor washed his own hands before the crowd and declared, "I am innocent of the blood of this just person" (Matthew 27:24).

The word *just* as applied to Jesus by Pilate and his wife means "innocent." Jesus, the sinless and righteous One, was not guilty of any crime or wrongdoing. This makes His death on our behalf all the more meaningful. He willingly laid down His life on the cross as the sacrifice for our sin.

Learn More: Luke 23:47 / Acts 3:14; 7:52; 22:14

KEEPER

*The LORD is thy keeper: the LORD
is thy shade upon thy right hand.*
PSALM 121:5

This is the only place in the Bible where God is referred to as our "keeper." This name refers to His protection, provision, and watchfulness. The New International Version renders the meaning of the name as "the LORD watches over you."

No matter where we are or what we are doing, God has His watchful eye on us. This can be either comforting or disturbing. As the writer of Proverbs said, "The eyes of the LORD are in every place, beholding the evil and the good" (Proverbs 15:3).

Just as God promises to keep us in His care, so we as believers are instructed to stay close to Him and keep His commandments. Psalm 119, the longest chapter in the Bible, pays tribute to God's written Word. It is filled with vows from the psalmist to stay true to God's commands in the Bible. "Give me understanding, and I shall keep thy law," he declared. "Yea, I shall observe it with my whole heart" (Psalm 119:34).

Learn More: Psalm 17:8; 25:20; 34:15; 91:11

KING ETERNAL, IMMORTAL, INVISIBLE

*Now unto the King eternal, immortal,
invisible, the only wise God, be honour
and glory for ever and ever. Amen.*
1 TIMOTHY 1:17

This benediction from the apostle Paul, in his first letter to Timothy, is the only place in the Bible where God is called by this name. The adjectives "eternal, immortal, invisible" express three of God's characteristics, or attributes.

God is eternal because He has always existed—and He always will. Unlike man, who is mortal, God is not subject to sickness and death. And He is invisible because He is a spiritual being who exists everywhere at the same time (John 4:24).

The prophet Jeremiah also referred to God as the "everlasting king" (Jeremiah 10:10). Both he and Paul were familiar with earthly kings who ruled for a few years, then were succeeded by other members of the royal family. Even the long reign of fifty-five years achieved by King Manasseh of Judah (2 Kings 21:1) is like the blink of an eye when compared to God's eternal kingship over the nations of the world.

Learn More: Deuteronomy 33:27 / John 4:23 / Romans 1:20 / 2 Corinthians 4:18 / 1 Timothy 6:16 / Colossians 1:15 / Hebrews 11:27

KING OF GLORY

Lift up your heads, O ye gates;
and be ye lift up, ye everlasting doors;
and the King of glory shall come in.
PSALM 24:7

Psalm 24 is the only place in the Bible where God is called the "King of glory," and the name appears five times in its ten verses. The title of the psalm ascribes it to David.

The exuberant joy of Psalm 24 leads some interpreters to speculate that it may have been sung when the ark of the covenant was moved to the city of Jerusalem in David's time. On this occasion David danced in celebration as trumpets sounded and the people shouted with joy (2 Samuel 6:14–16).

Two choirs, singing responsively, may have accompanied the ark. One choir sang, "Who is this King of glory?" And the other choir responded by identifying Him as Yahweh, the strong and mighty God of the Israelites.

As the King of glory, God is worthy of our praise. The psalmist declared, "Not unto us, O LORD, not unto us, but unto thy name give glory" (Psalm 115:1).

Learn More: Psalm 29:3 / Daniel 2:37 / 1 Corinthians 2:8

KING OF KINGS

*And he hath on his vesture and on his thigh a
name written, KING OF KINGS AND LORD OF LORDS.*
REVELATION 19:16

Chapter 19 of the book of Revelation describes the return
of Christ to earth in the end time. According to this verse,
He will wear a banner emblazoned with the phrase "King of
kings." This name, emphasizing His supreme rule over all the
earth, will be prominently displayed for everyone to see.

In Old Testament times, the title "king of kings" was
assigned to a ruler with an empire that covered a wide
territory. Often a king of an empire would allow the rulers
of conquered nations to keep their royal titles for political
and economic reasons. But it was clear that he as "king of
kings" was the undisputed ruler of his vast domain. Thus,
the Persian ruler Artaxerxes referred to himself as "king
of kings" in a letter that he sent to Jerusalem with Ezra the
priest (Ezra 7:12).

When Jesus returns in glory, He will be the sole ruler
of the universe. Meanwhile, He rules over His kingdom
known as the church. If we belong to Him, we are subjects
of His kingdom. He is the King of kings over our lives.

Learn More: Psalm 89:27; 102:15 / Zechariah 14:9 /
Revelation 17:14

And Jesus stood before the governor: and the
governor asked him, saying, Art thou the King of
the Jews? And Jesus said unto him, Thou sayest.
MATTHEW 27:11

This question of Pontius Pilate, the Roman governor who condemned Jesus to death, appears in all four Gospels (see also Mark 15:12; Luke 23:3; John 18:33). The Gospel writers considered this name important because it was the basis of the charge that led to Jesus' execution.

The Jewish religious leaders who turned Jesus over to Pilate were enraged by what they considered blasphemy, His claim to be the Son of God (Matthew 26:63–66). But they knew the Romans would never condemn Jesus to death on the basis of their religious laws alone (John 18:29–32). So they claimed that Jesus was guilty of sedition against the Roman government by claiming to be a king (Luke 23:2). The implication of this charge was that Jesus was plotting to overthrow Roman rule.

Jesus refused to answer Pilate's question because He knew the time for His sacrificial death had arrived. He would allow events to run their course without protest because it was His destiny to die on the cross. Jesus would sacrifice Himself willingly to provide salvation for the entire world.

Learn More: Matthew 2:2 / John 1:49; 12:13

LAMB OF GOD

The next day John seeth Jesus coming unto him, and saith, Behold the Lamb of God, which taketh away the sin of the world.
JOHN 1:29

Of all the names John the Baptist could have used for Jesus, he chose to identify Him as the "Lamb of God." Lambs were choice young sheep used as sacrificial animals in Jewish worship rituals (Leviticus 14:11–13). Thus, here at the very beginning of Jesus' ministry, John realized the sacrificial role Jesus was destined to fill.

The use of lambs as sacrifices began with the deliverance of the Israelites from slavery in Egypt. The Lord commanded the people to smear the blood of lambs on the doorposts of their houses. This indicated that they would be passed over when God struck the land with the death of the firstborn (Exodus 12:21–23).

On the night before His crucifixion, Jesus picked up on the sacrificial lamb imagery. He gathered His disciples for a meal that was part of the observance of the Jewish festival of Passover. As Jesus passed the cup among the disciples, He told them, "This is my blood of the new testament, which is shed for many for the remission of sins" (Matthew 26:28).

Learn More: Ephesians 2:13 / Hebrews 9:12 / 1 Peter 1:18–19 / 1 John 1:7

LAST ADAM

*The first man Adam was made a living soul;
the last Adam was made a quickening spirit.*
1 CORINTHIANS 15:45

The apostle Paul in this verse drew a contrast between Jesus as the "last Adam" and the Adam of the book of Genesis who was the first man created. This contrast appears at several points throughout the fifteenth chapter of 1 Corinthians.

After God placed the man in the garden of Eden, He told Adam that he could eat the fruit from every tree in the garden except one—"the tree of the knowledge of good and evil" (Genesis 2:17). But Adam disobeyed God and ate the forbidden fruit anyway (Genesis 3:6). This act of rebellion placed Adam and all his descendants—everyone born since Adam's time—under the curse of sin and death.

But there was good news for those who were tainted by Adam's sin. God sent another Adam—the last Adam, Jesus Christ—to undo what the first Adam had caused. The apostle Paul expressed it like this: "As in Adam all die, even so in Christ shall all be made alive" (1 Corinthians 15:22). The first Adam's legacy of death has been canceled by the last Adam's perfect obedience to God the Father, and His sacrificial death on our behalf.

Learn More: Genesis 2:19 / Job 31:33 / Romans 5:14

LAWGIVER

For the LORD is our judge, the LORD is our lawgiver, the LORD is our king; he will save us.

ISAIAH 33:22

This name of the Lord reflects His delivery of the Ten Commandments to Moses on Mount Sinai (Exodus 20:1–17). There was no doubt about the divine origin of these laws, because they were "written with the finger of God" (Exodus 31:18).

These commandments were a moral code to guide the behavior of God's people, the Israelites, whom He had delivered from slavery in Egypt. The Lord is sovereign over His creation, and He is the source of truth, righteousness, and holiness. He alone has the authority to make the laws and set the standards by which His people should live.

Many people have a strictly negative view of God's laws. They think of them only in binding and restrictive terms. But these laws are actually given for our benefit: following God's directives and commands is the key to joy and contentment in life. The psalmist focused on this positive side of God's laws when he declared, "Thou art good, and doest good; teach me thy statutes" (Psalm 119:68).

Learn More: Nehemiah 9:13 / Psalm 105:45 / Daniel 9:10 / Hebrews 8:10 / James 4:12

LIFE

When Christ, who is our life, shall appear,
then shall ye also appear with him in glory.
COLOSSIANS 3:4

We are accustomed to thinking of Jesus in terms of the eternal life that He promises to believers. But in this verse from the apostle Paul's letter to the Colossian believers, he describes Jesus as the "life" of believers in the here-and-now. In the previous verse, Paul declared that the Colossians had been trapped hopelessly in their sin before Christ gave them a glorious new life as His followers.

The message of this divine name is that we don't have to wait until we die to enjoy life with Jesus. He is our life today—in this present world. The apostle John stated it like this: "The Word gave life to everything that was created, and his life brought light to everyone" (John 1:4 NLT).

With Jesus as our life, we can live each day with joy in spite of the problems and frustrations that come our way. He is the very essence of the truly good life, and He promises the same to those who follow Him. Jesus himself declared, "I am come that they might have life, and that they might have it more abundantly" (John 10:10).

Learn More: John 1:4; 20:31 / Acts 3:14–15 / 1 John 1:1

LIGHT OF ISRAEL

And the light of Israel shall be for a fire, and
his Holy One for a flame: and it shall burn and
devour his thorns and his briers in one day.
ISAIAH 10:17

This name of God was used by the prophet Isaiah in connection with his prophecy about the nation of Assyria. The Assyrians overran the nation of Israel (the northern Jewish kingdom) about 722 BC. Isaiah predicted that Assyria would eventually be punished by the Lord for their mistreatment of His people. God—the "light of Israel"—would become a blazing fire that would consume this pagan nation. This prophecy was fulfilled about a century after Isaiah's time when Assyria fell to the Babylonians.

These images of light and fire show two different sides of God's nature. It is always better to experience the light of His love than the fire of His wrath.

This imagery of the light of Israel was also applied by Simeon to the infant Jesus at His dedication in the temple. Simeon described Jesus as "a light to lighten the Gentiles, and the glory of thy people Israel" (Luke 2:32).

Learn More: Exodus 13:21 / 2 Kings 8:19 / 2 Chronicles 21:7 / Psalm 27:1 / Isaiah 60:19 / John 8:12

LIGHT OF THE WORLD

Then spake Jesus again unto them,
saying, I am the light of the world:
he that followeth me shall not walk in
darkness, but shall have the light of life.
JOHN 8:12

The Jewish religious leaders to whom Jesus addressed this comment were filled with pride. They thought of God's favor on the Jewish people as something they deserved because of their moral superiority. But they forgot that God had blessed them because He wanted them to serve as His witnesses to the rest of the world.

Jesus was sent by God the Father as a Savior for all people. This is one reason He was rejected by the religious elite of His time. How could God the Father possibly love the pagan peoples of the world as much as He loved the Jewish leadership? They wanted to put limits on God's love and concern.

This problem is still with us today. Some people want to make Jesus into the light of the middle class, or the light of Western society, or the light of the beautiful. But He refuses to be bound by such restrictions. He is also the light of the poor, the light of the Third World, and the light of the homely. No matter what your earthly circumstances, He is *your* light.

Learn More: Genesis 1:3 / Isaiah 42:6 / John 1:6–7; 9:5

LION OF THE TRIBE OF JUDAH

*Behold, the Lion of the tribe of Judah, the Root
of David, hath prevailed to open the book,
and to loose the seven seals thereof.*
REVELATION 5:5

This verse declares that only Jesus, as "the Lion of the tribe of Judah," is worthy to open the scroll that contains God's end-time judgment against the world. This name of Jesus probably reflects a prophecy of Jacob in the book of Genesis: he declared that his son Judah was destined to become the greatest among all his twelve sons, whose descendants would become the Israelites, God's chosen people. Jacob described Judah symbolically as a lion, a fearless ruler, who would lead God's people (Genesis 49:8–12).

This prophecy was fulfilled dramatically throughout the Bible. The tribe of Judah took the lead on the Israelites' trek through the wilderness after they left Egypt (Numbers 10:14). Moses' census of the people in the wilderness revealed that the tribe of Judah was the largest of the twelve (Numbers 26:22).

Most significantly of all, Jesus the Messiah sprang from the line of Judah. The genealogy of Jesus in the Gospel of Matthew traces His lineage back to Judah (Matthew 1:2–3; *Judas*: KJV). Thus Jesus is the Lion of the tribe of Judah who rules among His people as supreme Savior and Lord.

Learn More: Numbers 1:26–27 / Psalm 78:67–72

LIVING GOD

And the king spake and said to Daniel,
O Daniel, servant of the living God,
is thy God, whom thou servest continually,
able to deliver thee from the lions?
DANIEL 6:20

King Darius of Persia was one of several people who used this name for the Lord. It was spoken when Darius went to the lion's den to see if Daniel had survived the night among the ferocious animals. Even a pagan king recognized that it would take the "living God" to deliver Daniel from this holding pen that had been turned into an execution chamber.

God is referred to as the *living* God several times throughout the Bible (Joshua 3:10; 1 Samuel 17:26; Jeremiah 10:10; Hebrews 10:31). This title contrasts the one true God—the One who actually exists—with pagan idols that are lifeless counterfeits. The prophet Isaiah claimed that the pagan deities of the ancient world were not gods at all but "the work of men's hands, wood and stone" that could be easily destroyed (Isaiah 37:19).

Unlike pagan deities, the living God is capable of acting on behalf of His people. Just as He saved Daniel from the lions, He hears our prayers and stands beside us in our times of need.

Learn More: Deuteronomy 5:26 / Psalm 42:2 / Daniel 6:26 / Romans 9:26

LIVING STONE

*To whom coming, as unto a living
stone, disallowed indeed of men,
but chosen of God, and precious.*
1 PETER 2:4

In this verse the apostle Peter compared Jesus to a stone used in the construction of a building. The imagery of a stone is applied to Jesus in other New Testament passages. But Peter referred to Jesus here as a "living stone," emphasizing His resurrection from the dead and His close relationship with believers as the living Christ.

Peter went on in the next verse to describe believers as "lively stones" (1 Peter 2:5). Just as Jesus is the living and breathing Head of the church, so believers make up the body of the church. Thus the church is a living organism devoted to the service of Jesus and His kingdom.

Peter summarized the mission of the church by stating that believers are "a chosen generation, a royal priesthood, an holy nation, a peculiar people; that ye should shew forth the praises of him who hath called you out of darkness into his marvellous light" (1 Peter 2:9).

We who belong to Jesus have the spirit of the "living stone" in our lives. We bring honor to Him when we serve as "lively stones" in the world.

Learn More: Psalm 118:22 / Matthew 21:42 /
Ephesians 2:19–20 / 1 Peter 2:7

LORD

*Therefore, my beloved brethren, be ye stedfast,
unmoveable, always abounding in the work of
the Lord, forasmuch as ye know that your
labour is not in vain in the Lord.*
1 CORINTHIANS 15:58

Sometimes the name *Lord* was used of Jesus as a term of respect. For example, a man once told Him, "Lord, I will follow thee whithersoever thou goest" (Luke 9:57). This man respected Jesus, but he did not reply when Jesus told him about the sacrifice He required of His followers (Luke 9:58).

Even Jesus' disciples sometimes called Him "Lord" in this polite, respectful sense. For example, Jesus once told a parable about the need for people to watch expectantly for His return. Peter asked Him, "Lord, speakest thou this parable unto us, or even to all?" (Luke 12:41).

As Jesus' earthly ministry unfolded, the polite title *Lord* that people used of Him was transformed into a declaration of faith in Him as the divine son of God. This is the sense in which the apostle Paul called Jesus "Lord" in the verse above.

After His resurrection and ascension, Jesus became the Lord of history, the Lord of the church, and the Lord of individual believers. When we declare that "Jesus is Lord," we submit to His leadership and crown Him as the supreme ruler over our lives.

Learn More: Romans 5:21 / Ephesians 5:8 /
1 Thessalonians 3:12

LORD GOD OF ISRAEL

Blessed be the Lord God of Israel; for
he hath visited and redeemed his people,
and hath raised up an horn of salvation
for us in the house of his servant David.
LUKE 1:68–69

Zacharias, the father of John the Baptist, used this name for God. It was part of his song of praise at the news that the Messiah would soon be born. Just as the Lord had blessed His people in the past, He was getting ready to fulfill His promise to send a great Deliverer.

Israel's gift to the world was belief in one universal God—a concept known as monotheism. The pagan peoples of the ancient world believed that many gods existed, with small deities ruling over different dimensions of life such as fire, war, and fertility. But the Israelites affirmed their belief in God and the ethical behavior He demanded in a formula known as the Shema: "Hear, O Israel: The LORD our God is one LORD: And thou shalt love the LORD thy God with all thine heart, and with all thy soul, and with all thy might" (Deuteronomy 6:4–5).

This Messiah from the Lord mentioned in Zacharias's song was more than a gift to Israel alone. Through Jesus the entire world would be blessed by His redemptive sacrifice on the cross.

Learn More: Exodus 32:27 / Psalm 41:13; 106:48

LORD OF HOSTS

*Yea, many people and strong nations shall
come to seek the L<small>ORD</small> of hosts in Jerusalem,
and to pray before the L<small>ORD</small>.*
ZECHARIAH 8:22

Zechariah 8 could be called the "Lord of Hosts" chapter of the Bible, because this divine name appears eighteen times within it. Actually, this name is one of the most popular in the entire Bible. It appears about 250 times, particularly in the prophets and the Psalms.

The compound Hebrew word behind this name is Yahweh-sabaoth, "Lord of Hosts." *Sabaoth* means "armies" or "hosts." Thus one meaning of the name is that God is superior to any human army, no matter its number. The Lord often led His people to victory over superior military forces (see, for example, Judges 7:12–25).

Another possible meaning of "Lord of Hosts" is that God exercises control over all the hosts of heaven—the heavenly bodies—including the sun, moon, and stars. The psalmist declared, "Praise ye him, all his hosts. Praise ye him, sun and moon: praise him, all ye stars of light" (Psalm 148:2–3).

In the King James Version, the title Lord of Sabaoth appears two times (Romans 9:29; James 5:4). These are rendered as "Lord of Hosts" by some modern translations.

Learn More: 1 Samuel 1:11 / Psalm 46:7 / Isaiah 5:16 / Jeremiah 25:32

LORD OF PEACE

Now the Lord of peace himself give you peace
always by all means. The Lord be with you all.
2 Thessalonians 3:16

As the apostle Paul ended his second letter to the Thessalonian believers, he blessed them with this beautiful benediction. Paul wanted these Christians, who were going through disagreement and turmoil, to experience the peace that Jesus promises to those who abide in Him.

The dictionary defines *peace* as "freedom from disquieting or oppressive thoughts or emotions." This definition assumes that peace is the *absence* of elements such as conflict or negative feelings. But we as believers know that peace is actually the *presence* of something greater. This presence is Jesus Christ, who brings peace and inner tranquility to those who have placed their trust in Him. With Jesus as the "Lord of peace" in our lives, we can have peace even in the midst of troubling circumstances.

When Jesus was born in Bethlehem, the angels celebrated His arrival by declaring "peace, good will toward men" (Luke 2:14). Jesus would one day tell His disciples, "Let not your heart be troubled: ye believe in God, believe also in me" (John 14:1). We don't have to go around with troubled looks on our faces if the Lord of peace reigns in our hearts.

Learn More: Isaiah 9:6 / Romans 16:20 / Ephesians 2:14 / Hebrews 13:20

LORD OF THE DEAD AND LIVING

*Whether we live therefore, or die, we are
the Lord's. For to this end Christ both died,
and rose, and revived, that he might be
Lord both of the dead and living.*
ROMANS 14:8–9

In this verse from Paul's letter to the believers at Rome, he referred to every individual who knew Christ as Lord and Savior. Jesus is Lord of the millions of Christians who have lived in the past and have now passed on to their heavenly reward. He is also Lord of all believers still living who look forward to eternal life with Him in heaven after their days on earth are over.

Whether we are alive or dead, there is no better place to be than in the hands of our loving Lord. This is the promise Jesus made to all believers just before He purchased our salvation through His redemptive death: "And I give unto them eternal life; and they shall never perish, neither shall any man pluck them out of my hand" (John 10:28).

Learn More: John 3:16 / Romans 6:23 / 2 Corinthians 5:15

LORD OF THE HARVEST

Pray ye therefore the Lord of the harvest, that
he will send forth labourers into his harvest.
MATTHEW 9:38

Jesus spoke these words to His disciples regarding the crowds who came to Him for healing and instruction. He was moved with compassion when He saw their need. Jesus longed for more workers to help Him, as the "Lord of the harvest," with the people problems that pressed in from every side.

Jesus had unlimited power, so why didn't He just take care of these difficulties Himself? Why tell the disciples to pray for more workers? Perhaps it was because He knew His time on earth was limited. Even if Jesus healed all the sick and taught everyone who followed Him, others in the same condition would take their place after He was gone. He needed committed workers who would carry on His work after His earthly ministry came to an end.

Jesus is still in the harvesting business. His work on earth continues through His church, and He still needs workers to gather the harvest. Our genuine concern for others should cause us to pray for them, and then work to bring them into God's kingdom. As the apostle Paul expressed it, "All things are of God, who hath reconciled us to himself by Jesus Christ, and hath given to us the ministry of reconciliation" (2 Corinthians 5:18).

Learn More: Matthew 13:30 / Luke 10:2 / John 4:35

LORD OF THE SABBATH

And he said unto them, The sabbath was made
for man, and not man for the sabbath. Therefore
the Son of man is Lord also of the sabbath.
MARK 2:27–28

This is how Jesus answered the Pharisees when they criticized Him for picking grain on the sabbath to feed Himself and the hungry disciples. The original law about sabbath observance stated simply, "Remember the sabbath day, to keep it holy" (Exodus 20:8). People were restricted from working on this day.

Over the years the Pharisees had added many human traditions to this simple law. For example, people were not to travel more than half a mile—or a "sabbath's day journey" (Acts 1:12)—on this day. These silly rules had reduced the sabbath from a spiritual principle to a meaningless ritual.

When Jesus claimed to be the "Lord of the Sabbath," He declared that He would not be bound by the human rules that the Pharisees had established. To Him, doing good on the sabbath by healing people was more important than obeying the religious leaders' silly rules (Matthew 12:12).

Jesus' claim to be the Lord of the Sabbath also placed Him on the same level as God the Father. God had established the sabbath, with Jesus as the agent of creation (John 1:1–3). This gave Him authority over the sabbath.

Learn More: Genesis 2:2–3 / Matthew 12:8 / Luke 6:5–11

LORD OUR RIGHTEOUSNESS

Israel shall dwell safely: and this is his name whereby he shall be called, THE LORD OUR RIGHTEOUSNESS.
JEREMIAH 23:6

God the Father delivered this message through the prophet Jeremiah. The Lord would punish His people for their sin by allowing them to be defeated by the Babylonians. But He would preserve a remnant who would remain faithful. God would bless them, eventually allow them to return to their homeland, and give them a special name—"The Lord Our Righteousness."

This name of God emphasizes two of the most important truths of the Bible: The Lord demands righteousness of His people, and we are not able to meet this demand on our own. He as the Lord Our Righteousness must provide righteousness on our behalf.

The ultimate fulfillment of this verse happened several centuries after Jeremiah's time. God sent His own Son into the world to pay the price for our sin so we could become justified, or righteous, in His sight. This is strictly a gift of God's grace, not something that we deserve because we measure up to His demands. The apostle Paul declared that God made Jesus "to be sin for us, who knew no sin; that we might be made the righteousness of God in him" (2 Corinthians 5:21).

Learn More: Psalm 4:1; 96:13 / Isaiah 45:19; 54:17

LORD OVER ALL

*For there is no difference between the
Jew and the Greek: for the same Lord
over all is rich unto all that call upon him.*

ROMANS 10:12

This name of Jesus may seem to express the same idea as Lord of lords (Revelation 19:16). But there is an important distinction between these two names.

Lord of lords refers to Jesus' supreme rule throughout the earth at His second coming. Lord Over All declares that all people are on the same level in relationship to Jesus Christ. Jesus does not have one plan of salvation for the Jewish people and another for Greeks, or non-Jews. Everyone comes to salvation by accepting through faith the price He paid to redeem us from our sin.

The Jews looked upon Greeks, or Gentiles, as pagans who were excluded from God's favor. The learned Greeks, in turn, thought of all people who were not Greek citizens as uncultured barbarians. But Paul declared that Jesus wiped out all such distinctions between people. Everyone stood before God as sinners with no hope except the forgiveness they could experience through Jesus' sacrifice.

Paul also made it clear that something is required of sinners who desire this salvation. They must "call upon" Jesus (Romans 10:13). This involves repenting of their sins, confessing Him as Savior, and committing their lives to His lordship.

Learn More: Acts 10:28 / Romans 3:29 / 1 Corinthians 12:13 / James 3:17

LORD WHO HEALS

And [God] said, If thou wilt diligently hearken
to the voice of the LORD thy God. . .I will
put none of these diseases upon thee,
which I have brought upon the Egyptians:
for I am the LORD that healeth thee.
EXODUS 15:26

This is the only place in the Bible where God is called the Lord Who Heals. God used this name to describe Himself after He healed the bitter waters at Marah in the wilderness, making them safe for the Israelites to drink.

The healing power of God is often demonstrated in the Old Testament. For example, He healed Miriam of her leprosy (Numbers 12:10–15). He healed King Hezekiah of Judah of a mysterious illness (2 Kings 20:1–6). And He healed people in the wilderness after they were bitten by poisonous snakes (Numbers 21:5–9).

God is also portrayed in the Old Testament as the healer of the ultimate sickness—sin. The psalmist prayed, "LORD, be merciful unto me: heal my soul; for I have sinned against thee" (Psalm 41:4). In His earthly ministry, Jesus continued this ministry through compassionate healing of the sick and suffering, including those in bondage to sin.

Learn More: 1 Kings 17:22 / 2 Kings 4:34–35 / Mark 2:17; 5:41–42

LORD WHO SANCTIFIES

*Speak thou also unto the children of Israel,
saying, Verily my sabbaths ye shall keep:
for it is a sign between me and you throughout
your generations; that ye may know that
I am the LORD that doth sanctify you.*

EXODUS 31:13

God reminded the Israelites through Moses that the Sabbath was a special day that had been set apart, or sanctified, by Him (Genesis 2:3). His people were to honor this day by resting from their labors and praising Him through acts of worship.

Just as God set apart the seventh day of the week as a memorial to Him, so He sanctified the Israelites as a nation devoted to Him. As the Lord Who Sanctifies, He has the right to demand loyalty and commitment from His people. When God sets us apart for His special use, He also empowers us with the strength and ability to serve as His witnesses in the world.

The apostle Paul expressed every believer's commission to service like this: "I beseech you therefore, brethren, by the mercies of God, that ye present your bodies a living sacrifice, holy, acceptable unto God, which is your reasonable service" (Romans 12:1).

Learn More: Leviticus 20:8 / Ezekiel 20:12 / 1 Thessalonians 5:23

MAJESTY ON HIGH

Who being the brightness of his glory,
and the express image of his person. . .when
he had by himself purged our sins, sat down
on the right hand of the Majesty on high.
HEBREWS 1:3

This verse from the book of Hebrews refers to the ascension of Jesus. After His resurrection, Jesus spent forty days among His followers. Then He was "taken up" into heaven and "a cloud received him out of their sight" (Acts 1:9). Now in heaven, He is seated at the right hand of God His Father (Ephesians 1:20)—or, as the writer of Hebrews put it, next to the "Majesty on high."

This name of God is a poetic way of referring to His power and glory. He is incomparable in His excellence, magnificence, and splendor. King David expressed this truth in a profound way when He declared, "Thine, O LORD is the greatness, and the power, and the glory, and the victory, and the majesty: for all that is in the heaven and in the earth is thine" (1 Chronicles 29:11).

"Majesty on high" as a divine name appears only here in the Bible. The writer of Hebrews also spoke of God as the "Majesty in the heavens" (Hebrews 8:1).

Learn More: Psalm 29:4; 96:6; 104:1; 145:12 /
Colossians 3:1 / 1 Peter 3:22

MAKER

Shall mortal man be more just than God?
shall a man be more pure than his maker?
JOB 4:17

Eliphaz the Temanite, one of Job's three friends, referred to God by this name. Job had accused God of causing his suffering, even though Job thought himself innocent of any wrongdoing. To Eliphaz, a mere mortal such as Job had no right to question the actions of his Maker, the immortal One who did not have to explain His actions to anyone.

God's role as our Maker is similar to His acts as our Creator and provider. He brought the first man, Adam, into being and breathed into him the breath of life (Genesis 2:7). And God continues to provide the elements needed to sustain life in His universe. We owe our very lives to Him as our Maker.

The psalmist acknowledged this truth when he declared, "Know ye that the LORD he is God: it is he that hath made us, and not we ourselves; we are his people, and the sheep of his pasture" (Psalm 100:3). See also *Creator*.

Learn More: Job 36:3 / Isaiah 45:9 / Hosea 8:14

*He is despised and rejected of men; a man of
sorrows, and acquainted with grief. . . . Surely he
hath borne our griefs, and carried our sorrows.*
ISAIAH 53:3–4

The dictionary defines *sorrow* as a state of remorse over a
great loss. If we apply this definition to Isaiah's prophecy,
perhaps an alternative translation of this name of Jesus is in
order. Jesus was a "man of suffering" (as the New Revised
Standard Version says) more than a "man of sorrows."

Jesus was not immersed in regret over a loss. He was an
overcomer—a victorious person—in spite of the problems
He faced during His earthly ministry. Even the suffering
that led to His death was swallowed up in victory when He
drew His last breath and declared, "It is finished" (John
19:30). He had accomplished the purpose for which He
had been sent into the world.

Jesus' suffering on the cross was real. So is the pain that
we as believers feel when we are ridiculed for our faith. But
this should not drive us to despair. The Man of Suffering has
already "borne our griefs, and carried our sorrows" by dying
in our place. Jesus invites us to cast our cares on Him and
share in the victory He achieved on the cross.

Learn More: Matthew 16:21 / Acts 3:18 / Hebrews 2:10

MASTER

And call no man your father upon the
earth: for one is your Father, which is
in heaven. Neither be ye called masters:
for one is your Master, even Christ.
MATTHEW 23:9–10

This name that Jesus used of Himself appears in the famous "woe" chapter in which He condemned the Pharisees (Matthew 23). He was particularly critical of their hypocrisy and religious pride. They enjoyed being greeted with titles that recognized them for their standing in the community and their expertise in the Jewish law. But Jesus declared that He as God's Son was the only person who deserved the title of "Master."

The term used in this verse comes from a Greek word that means "commander" or "ruler." Modern translations sometimes render this word as "teacher." But Jesus was claiming to be more than a teacher. He made it clear to His disciples and others who were listening that He had the right to serve as the supreme authority in their lives.

In New Testament times, slave owners were sometimes called "masters" (Colossians 4:1), implying their total control over the lives of their subjects. As believers, we are also subject to the will of our Master, the Lord Jesus, who has redeemed us for His service.

Learn More: Matthew 6:24 / John 13:13 / Ephesians 6:9 / Colossians 4:1

MEDIATOR

*For there is one God, and one mediator
between God and men, the man Christ
Jesus; who gave himself a ransom for
all, to be testified in due time.*
1 TIMOTHY 2:5–6

A mediator is a "middleman" or "go-between" who brings two opposing parties together. In this verse, according to the apostle Paul, Jesus fills the role of spiritual mediator in the world. He is the in-between agent who reconciles humankind to God.

All people by nature are sinners. We are estranged from a holy God, who will not tolerate anything that is unholy or unclean. But Jesus eliminated this gap between God and humankind by sacrificing Himself for our sins and purchasing our forgiveness. Cleansed of our sin through His blood, we now have fellowship with God the Father. We have been reconciled to God through His work as our Mediator.

Jesus is the perfect Mediator because He had both divine and human attributes. As God, He understood what God the Father demanded of sinners in order to be acceptable in His sight. As a man, He realized the desperate situation of sinful human beings. Jesus was the God-man who was able to bring these two opposites together. Through His sinless life and perfect sacrifice, He glorified God and gave the human race access to God's unlimited blessings.

Learn More: 2 Corinthians 5:18 / Hebrews 8:6; 9:15; 12:24

MESSIAH

The woman saith unto him [Jesus], I know that
Messias cometh, which is called Christ: when he
is come, he will tell us all things. Jesus saith unto
her, I that speak unto thee am he.
JOHN 4:25–26

These two verses are part of Jesus' conversation with the Samaritan woman at the well. He admitted to her that He was the Messiah, the deliverer whom God had been promising to send to His people for hundreds of years.

The only other place in the New Testament where the word *Messiah* appears is also in John's Gospel. After meeting Jesus, Andrew told his brother, Simon Peter, "We have found the Messias" (John 1:41).

It's not surprising that the title Messiah appears rarely in the New Testament, because Jesus discouraged others from referring to Him in this way (Matthew 16:20). The Jewish people expected their messiah to be a political and military deliverer who would throw off the yoke of Rome and restore the fortunes of Israel. Jesus had come into the world as the spiritual Messiah, so He avoided this name because it would lead the people to expect Him to be something He was not.

Though the word *Messiah* is rare in the New Testament, the concept appears often. The Greek term *christos*, rendered as "Christ," means "anointed" or "anointed one"—a word referring to the Messiah or God's Chosen One.

Learn More: Daniel 9:25–26

*I will feed them that oppress thee with
their own flesh. . .and all flesh shall know
that I the LORD am thy Saviour and thy
Redeemer, the mighty One of Jacob.*

ISAIAH 49:26

This name of God appears only twice in the Bible, both times in the book of Isaiah (see Isaiah 60:16). In these two verses, "Jacob" is a poetic way of referring to the nation of Israel. The descendants of Jacob's twelve sons developed into the twelve tribes that made up the nation of Israel. Jacob himself was also known as "Israel," a name given to him by the Lord after his struggle with God at Peniel (Genesis 32:28; 35:10).

Jacob, the grandson of Abraham, was a schemer who deceived his father, Isaac, into blessing him rather than his twin brother, Esau. But over time he developed into a person who honored the Lord and became heir to the covenant that God had established with Abraham.

Three divine names similar to "mighty One of Jacob" that appear in the Old Testament are "God of Jacob" (2 Samuel 23:1), "Holy One of Jacob" (Isaiah 29:23), and "King of Jacob" (Isaiah 41:21).

Learn More: Genesis 27:1–41; 32:27–28

MINISTER OF THE TRUE TABERNACLE

*We have such an high priest, who is set
on the right hand of the throne of the
Majesty in the heavens; a minister of the
sanctuary, and of the true tabernacle.*
HEBREWS 8:1–2

In this verse the writer of Hebrews claims that the Old Testament priestly system was only a shadow of the eternal priesthood provided by Jesus in heaven. He is the priest of the heavenly sanctuary, or true tabernacle, that God has established for His people.

The most holy place in the Jewish religious system was the "holy of holies" in the tabernacle or temple. This sanctuary represented God's holy and awesome presence. Only the high priest could enter this section of the temple, and he could do so only once a year on the Day of Atonement. On this occasion, he offered sacrifice first for his own sins and then for the sins of the people (Leviticus 16:1–6).

When Jesus died on the cross, the heavy curtain that sealed off this section of the temple was torn from top to bottom (Matthew 27:50–51). This symbolized that all people now had access to God's presence and forgiveness through the sacrificial death of His Son.

Jesus is the perfect priest in heaven, where He conducts His ministry of intercession for all believers (Hebrews 7:25).

Learn More: Exodus 40:12–15 / Matthew 20:28 / Mark 10:43 / Romans 15:8

MOST HIGH

The LORD thundered from heaven,
and the most High uttered his voice.
2 SAMUEL 22:14

This name of God appears in a psalm that David wrote after he was delivered from King Saul and others who were trying to kill him (1 Samuel 20:1; Psalm 18 title). David compared God's ability to save to the power unleashed during a severe thunderstorm. The rolling thunder was like God's voice from heaven. Anyone who has ever been caught outside during a sudden storm can testify to the awesome power of nature and its Creator.

The name "most High" appears primarily in the Old Testament. One exception occurs in Stephen's long speech in the book of Acts. This early Christian martyr declared that "the most High dwelleth not in temples made with hands" (Acts 7:48).

There is nothing in this world more powerful than the most High. The only appropriate response to displays of His power in the universe is to bow down and worship. As the psalmist declared, "O worship the LORD in the beauty of holiness: fear before him, all the earth" (Psalm 96:9).

Learn More: Psalm 9:2; 73:11; 107:11 / Isaiah 14:14 / Daniel 4:24; 7:18

NEW SPIRIT

*A new heart also will I give you, and a new
spirit will I put within you: and I will take
away the stony heart out of your flesh,
and I will give you an heart of flesh.*

EZEKIEL 36:26

Just as Jeremiah is known as the prophet of the new
covenant (Jeremiah 31:31–34), Ezekiel might be called the
prophet of the "new spirit." This name of the Holy Spirit
is unique to him, and he uses it three times in his book
(see also Ezekiel 11:19; 18:31).

The word *new* does not mean that God would give His
people the Holy Spirit for the first time at some point in the
future. The Holy Spirit was active with God the Father in the
creation and among selected people in Old Testament times,
including Joshua, Othniel the judge, Samson, and David.
The name "new spirit" refers to the spiritual redemption
that God would provide for His people through His love
and grace. God's Spirit would bind believers to Him in a
new covenant sealed with the blood of Jesus Christ.

Learn More: Numbers 27:18 / Judges 3:9–10; 14:5–6 /
1 Samuel 16:13 / 2 Corinthians 3:6

ONE CHOSEN OUT OF THE PEOPLE

Then thou spakest in vision to thy holy one, and
saidst, I have laid help upon one that is mighty;
I have exalted one chosen out of the people.
PSALM 89:19

Psalm 89 focuses on God's promise to King David that one of his descendants would always occupy the throne of Israel (2 Samuel 7:8–17). Thus the "one chosen out of the people" in this verse refers to David, because he was chosen by the Lord from among the sons of Jesse to replace Saul as king (1 Samuel 16:10–13).

But this psalm also looks beyond David's time to its ultimate fulfillment in Jesus the Messiah. The angel Gabriel made this clear when he told the virgin Mary that she would give birth to God's Chosen One. "He shall be great, and shall be called the Son of the Highest," Gabriel declared, "and the Lord God shall give unto him the throne of his father David" (Luke 1:32).

As the one chosen out of the people, Jesus was not a king in the same sense as David. He did not seek political or military power. His kingship was spiritual in nature. Jesus ushered in the kingdom of God, the dominion over which He reigns with all who have accepted Him as Lord and Savior.

Learn More: Psalm 135:4 / Isaiah 42:1 / 1 Peter 2:4

*For God so loved the world, that he gave his
only begotten Son, that whosoever believeth in
him should not perish, but have everlasting life.*

JOHN 3:16

Jesus used this name for Himself in His long discussion with Nicodemus about the meaning of the new birth (John 3:1–21). This verse from that discussion is probably the best known passage in the entire Bible. Most believers can quote it from memory. It has been called "the Gospel in a nutshell" because its twenty-five words tell so clearly and simply why Jesus came into the world.

The name "only begotten Son" describes Jesus' special relationship with the Father. He is unique—the only one of His kind who has ever existed. The fact that He was God's one and only Son makes His role as our Savior all the more significant. God the Father sent the very best when He sent Jesus to die for our sins.

This name of Jesus appears only in the writings of the apostle John. In his Gospel, John also referred to Jesus as the "only begotten of the Father" (John 1:14).

Learn More: Psalm 2:7 / John 1:18; 3:18 / 1 John 4:9 / Hebrews 1:5

ONLY WISE GOD

*Now unto him that is able to keep you
from falling, and to present you faultless
before the presence of his glory with
exceeding joy, to the only wise God our
Saviour, be glory and majesty, dominion
and power, both now and for ever. Amen.*

JUDE 24–25

The writer of the epistle of Jude closed his brief book with this inspiring benediction. He wanted his readers to experience the joy of their salvation and to continue to be faithful to the "only wise God," whom he clearly identified as Jesus their Savior.

This is the only place in the Bible where Jesus is called by this name. The New King James Version translates the phrase as "God our Savior, who alone is wise." Only Jesus Christ has divine wisdom. Worldly wisdom is a poor substitute for the wisdom that God grants those who follow Him as Savior and Lord.

Jesus the Son and God the Father impart wisdom to believers in several ways—through the Holy Spirit, through the counsel of fellow believers, and through the scriptures, the written Word of God. We will never be as wise as God, who is the fount of all wisdom. But we should be growing in this gift of grace every day as we walk with Him.

Learn More: Matthew 11:25 / 1 Corinthians 1:24 / James 1:5

OUR PASSOVER

*Purge out therefore the old leaven, that ye may
be a new lump, as ye are unleavened. For even
Christ our passover is sacrificed for us.*
1 CORINTHIANS 5:7

The festival of Passover commemorated the "passing over" of the houses of the Israelites when God destroyed all the Egyptian firstborn. This was God's final plague that convinced the pharaoh to release the Jewish people from slavery.

Jesus is "our passover," Paul declared, because He shed His blood to bring deliverance for God's people, just as sacrificial lambs inaugurated the first Passover. We remember Jesus' sacrifice with reverence every time we partake of communion, or the Lord's Supper.

The word *leaven* in this verse refers to yeast, an ingredient used by the Israelites to cause their bread to rise. On the first Passover, they left Egypt in such a hurry that they didn't have time to add leaven to their bread dough (Exodus 12:34). Whenever they observed this holiday from that day on, they were to eat unleavened bread.

Paul referred to believers in this verse as a "new lump" because they were "unleavened." Just as unleavened bread symbolized the Israelites' freedom from Egyptian slavery, so believers are unleavened, or separated from sin and death, by the perfect Passover Lamb, Jesus Christ.

Learn More: 2 Kings 23:21 / Matthew 26:2 / Mark 14:1

*And Jesus answering said unto them,
They that are whole need not a
physician; but they that are sick.*
LUKE 5:31

Jesus spoke these words soon after He called the tax collector Matthew as His disciple. To celebrate the occasion, Matthew invited his tax collector associates and other friends to a meal for Jesus and the other disciples.

The scribes and Pharisees were horrified that Jesus and His disciples would associate with such "sinful" people. But Jesus made it clear that He had been sent to people such as these. They needed a Savior and Deliverer. He was the Physician who could heal them of their desperate sickness known as sin.

Jesus' role as physician is one of the most prominent in the Gospels. Most of His miracles were performed for people who were suffering from physical ailments. But in many of these miracles, He went beyond healing the body to healing the soul and the spirit through forgiveness of sin (Matthew 9:2).

Jesus the Physician is still in the healing business. He offers hope to the discouraged, His presence to the lonely, comfort to the grieving, and peace to those who are troubled. But most of all, He brings deliverance from the most serious problems of the human race—sin and death.

Learn More: Matthew 4:23 / Mark 2:17 / Luke 5:31

PORTION

*Thou art my portion, O Lᴏʀᴅ: I have said
that I would keep thy words. I intreated thy
favour with my whole heart: be merciful
unto me according to thy word.*
Pꜱᴀʟᴍ 119:57–58

The word *portion* appears often in the Bible in connection with inheritance rights. For example, each of the twelve tribes of Israel received a portion of the land of Canaan as an inheritance that the Lord had promised (Joshua 19:9). By law, the firstborn son in a family received a double portion of his father's estate as an inheritance (Deuteronomy 21:17). In Jesus' parable of the prodigal son, the youngest son asked his father for his portion or share of the estate ahead of time (Luke 15:12).

The psalmist probably had this inheritance imagery in mind when he called God "my portion." The Lord was his spiritual heritage, passed down to him by godly people of past generations. Unlike an earthly inheritance that can be squandered, this is an inheritance that will last forever.

But comparing God to a legacy from the past has its limits. Truths about God can be passed on from generation to generation, but personal faith cannot. Parents can and should teach their offspring about God, but it is up to each child to accept this heritage through personal choice.

Learn More: Psalm 16:5; 119:57; 142:5 / Lamentations 3:24

POTTER

But now, O LORD, thou art our father;
we are the clay, and thou our potter;
and we all are the work of thy hand.

ISAIAH 64:8

The prophet Isaiah longed for the wayward people of Judah to return to the Lord. If they became pliable clay in God's hands, they would be shaped into beautiful vessels who would glorify His name.

God as the master potter is a graphic image that appears often throughout the Bible. For example, while the prophet Jeremiah looked on, a potter ruined a vase he was working on and had to start over again with the same lump of clay. Jeremiah compared the nation of Judah to this pottery reshaping process. Shape up, he declared, or you will be reshaped by the Lord's discipline.

In the New Testament, the apostle Paul observed that believers are nothing but "earthen vessels" (*jars of clay*, NIV), who are filled with the treasure of God's grace (2 Corinthians 4:7). But our unworthiness as recipients of His grace should not prevent us from serving as witnesses of His love to others.

Learn More: Jeremiah 18:2–6 / Revelation 2:27

But we preach Christ crucified, unto the Jews a stumblingblock, and unto the Greeks foolishness; but unto them which are called, both Jews and Greeks, Christ the power of God, and the wisdom of God.
1 CORINTHIANS 1:23–24

The apostle Paul admitted that many people were skeptical of a crucified Savior. If Jesus was such a deliverer, they reasoned, why was He executed on a Roman cross like a common criminal? To them, Jesus' death was a sign of weakness.

On the contrary, Paul pointed out, Christ showed great power in His crucifixion. He was the very "power of God" whom the Father sent to atone for the sins of the world. The death of One on behalf of the many showed the extent of this divine power.

Jesus demonstrated His awesome power many times during His earthly ministry. But He refused to come down from the cross and save Himself, although the crowd taunted Him to do so.

This is a good example of power under control. Jesus could have called legions of angels to come to His rescue. But this would have nullified the purpose for which God the Father had sent Him into the world. His divine power was never greater than when He refused to use it.

Learn More: Matthew 26:53; 27:39–43 / 1 Corinthians 2:5 / Ephesians 6:10 / 2 Timothy 1:8

POWER OF THE HIGHEST

*And the angel answered and said unto her,
The Holy Ghost shall come upon thee, and the
power of the Highest shall overshadow thee.*

LUKE 1:35

The angel Gabriel spoke these words of assurance to the virgin Mary. She would give birth to the Son of God. Jesus' conception in her womb would occur through the action of the Holy Spirit, whom Gabriel referred to as the "power of the Highest."

No other word describes the work of God's Spirit as well as *power*. In the Old Testament, King Saul experienced this firsthand when he sent several assassins to kill David. But the Spirit of God came upon them, causing them to utter prophecies instead of carrying out the king's orders (1 Samuel 19:20).

In the New Testament, Jesus told His disciples that the Holy Spirit would empower them to continue His mission in the world (Acts 1:8). The outpouring of the Holy Spirit on the day of Pentecost transformed the small group into bold witnesses for Jesus.

But the Holy Spirit's power is not restricted to that time long ago. He is still at work through the church and those who follow Jesus as Lord and Savior. This is possible "not by might, nor by power, but by my spirit, saith the LORD of hosts" (Zechariah 4:6).

Learn More: Acts 1:8; 2:1–11 / Romans 15:13

PRINCE OF THE KINGS OF THE EARTH

Grace be unto you, and peace. . .from
Jesus Christ, who is the faithful witness,
and the first begotten of the dead, and
the prince of the kings of the earth.
REVELATION 1:4–5

The apostle John addressed the book of Revelation to seven churches of Asia Minor whose members were undergoing persecution by Roman authorities. John wanted these believers to understand that he was not writing under his own authority but under the command and direction of Jesus Christ, the "prince of the kings of the earth."

Rulers like the emperors of the Roman Empire would come and go. But Jesus was an eternal King, not a temporary monarch who would rule for a few years, then be replaced by another. He stands above and beyond all the kings of the earth.

Since Jesus is the world's supreme King, He has the right to reign over His church and in the lives of those who claim Him as Savior and Lord. As the apostle Paul reminded the believers at Ephesus, "We are his workmanship, created in Christ Jesus unto good works, which God hath before ordained that we should walk in them" (Ephesians 2:10).

Learn More: Zechariah 14:9 / Acts 3:15; 5:31 / Revelation 19:16

PROPITIATION FOR OUR SINS

Herein is love, not that we loved God,
but that he loved us, and sent his Son
to be the propitiation for our sins.
1 JOHN 4:10

The word *propitiation* comes from an old English word that means "to satisfy." Thus, the apostle John declared that God the Father sent His Son, Jesus, to serve as the satisfaction for our sins. This word is the key to one of the classical theories of the atonement, or the sacrificial death of Jesus.

According to this view, God is a holy God who cannot tolerate sin. This puts us as humans in a dilemma because we are not capable of living a sinless life, no matter how hard we try. To make matters worse, God is also a just God who—in order to be true to His nature—must punish sin wherever He finds it. So our sin separates us from God and makes us liable to His punishment. *Hopeless* is the only word that describes the human situation.

But God loved us too much to allow us to continue in this dilemma. He sent Jesus to satisfy His own demand for righteousness in His people. Jesus sacrificed His life, atoned for our sins, and restored the broken relationship between a holy God and sinful humanity.

Learn More: Mark 10:45 / 1 Timothy 2:6 / 1 John 1:7 / Revelation 1:5

RABBI

The same [Nicodemus] came to Jesus by night, and said unto him, Rabbi, we know that thou art a teacher come from God: for no man can do these miracles that thou doest, except God be with him.
JOHN 3:2

In modern society, *rabbi* is the official title of the leader of a Jewish congregation. It is similar to the title *reverend* for a Protestant minister or *father* for a Catholic priest.

But in Jesus' time, *rabbi* was a term of respect meaning "teacher" or "master." In John 3:2, Nicodemus's use of this title for Jesus probably meant "teacher." Nicodemus wanted to learn more about this Jewish teacher and miracle worker who was impressing the crowds in the region of Galilee.

In John 20:16, Mary Magdalene's recognition of Jesus as "rabboni" paid homage to Him as her master. After Jesus' resurrection, Mary recognized Him as such when He called her by name. *Rabboni* is the Aramaic form of rabbi. Aramaic was the common language spoken in Israel during New Testament times.

Whether we call Jesus *Rabbi* or *Rabboni*, the meaning is the same: He is our Master, Teacher, and Guide who deserves our utmost respect and loyalty.

Learn More: John 1:38, 49; 6:25

REDEEMER

And the Redeemer shall come to
Zion, and unto them that turn from
transgression in Jacob, saith the LORD.
ISAIAH 59:20

This divine name is a reflection of the Old Testament concept of the kinsman-redeemer. In Bible times, a family member in trouble depended on his nearest relative to come to his rescue.

For example, if a person lost his property to a debtor, his kinsman-redeemer was responsible for buying it back and restoring it to this family member. This is what happened in the case of Naomi in the book of Ruth. Boaz, a kinsman of Naomi's deceased husband, bought back the property her husband had lost and restored it to her (Ruth 4:1–11).

The prophet Isaiah declared that God is the ultimate Redeemer who will come to the rescue of His people. The patriarch Job also received a glimpse of this Redeemer of the future. Out of his suffering and despair, Job declared, "I know that my redeemer liveth, and that he shall stand at the latter day upon the earth" (Job 19:25).

What Isaiah and Job only hoped for has now come to pass. We can rest assured that no trouble that we experience is so deep that it is beyond the reach of a loving Lord.

Learn More: Psalm 19:14 / Isaiah 49:7 / Jeremiah 50:34

REFINER'S FIRE

But who may abide the day of his coming?
and who shall stand when he appeareth?
for he is like a refiner's fire, and like fullers' soap.
MALACHI 3:2

This name of Jesus appears in the final chapter of the Old Testament. The prophet Malachi compared the coming Messiah to the hot fire that metalworkers used to purify ore such as silver. The ore was heated in a pot until it turned to liquid and the dross (waste material) rose to the surface. Then the metalworker used a ladle to skim off the dross, leaving the pure and uncontaminated silver.

This image of the Messiah must have been a surprise to the Jewish people of Malachi's time. They expected the Messiah to come as a conquering hero who would restore Israel to its glory days as a political kingdom. But the prophet informed them that the Messiah would come in judgment against Israel because of its sin and rebellion.

The name "refiner's fire" emphasizes Jesus' role as judge. His second coming will bring judgment against all who have refused to accept Him as Savior and Lord.

Learn More: Proverbs 17:3; 25:4 / Isaiah 1:25 / Ezekiel 22:22 / Malachi 3:3 / 2 Peter 2:9

REFUGE

*The eternal God is thy refuge, and underneath
are the everlasting arms: and he shall thrust
out the enemy from before thee.*
DEUTERONOMY 33:27

Moses called God by this name as the Israelites were getting ready to enter the promised land. He reminded the people to follow the Lord as they settled in the land because He alone was a dependable source of refuge and protection.

After they occupied Canaan, the Israelites designated certain population centers as cities of refuge (Joshua 20:7–9). An Israelite who killed another person accidentally could flee to one of these cities to escape the dead man's family who were seeking revenge. The person's safety was guaranteed by the elders of the city while the circumstances surrounding the death were under investigation.

With God as our refuge, we have nothing to fear from those who seek to do us harm. Even in death, there is no safer place to be than in the arms of the everlasting God. The psalmist declared, "I will say of the LORD, He is my refuge and my fortress: my God; in him will I trust" (Psalm 91:2).

Another divine name that emphasizes God's protection of His people is "hiding place" (Psalm 32:7).

Learn More: Numbers 35:12–15 / Psalm 46:1; 61:3; 142:5 / Jeremiah 16:19

RESURRECTION AND THE LIFE

Jesus said unto her [Martha], I am the
resurrection, and the life: he that believeth in
me, though he were dead, yet shall he live.
JOHN 11:25

Jesus applied this name to Himself while talking with Martha, sister of Lazarus. She was disappointed that Jesus had not arrived to heal her brother before he died. Jesus' reply made it clear that He was the master of the living and the dead. He had the power to raise Lazarus, as well as any others who had died. At the same time, He could guarantee eternal life for the living.

Then Jesus proceeded to deliver on His promise. He stood before the burial chamber where the body had been placed, and with the simple command, "Lazarus, come forth," brought His friend back to life.

Note that Jesus delivered no incantations over the body; there was no lightning flash from heaven, no magical tricks to dazzle the crowd. Just three simple words from the Master, and Lazarus walked out of the tomb.

Jesus alone has the keys to life and death. Fortunate are those who commit their lives and their eternal destiny into His hands.

Learn More: John 11:26 / Acts 4:33 / Philippians 3:10 / 1 Peter 1:3

He shall see of the travail of his soul,
and shall be satisfied: by his knowledge
shall my righteous servant justify many;
for he shall bear their iniquities.

ISAIAH 53:11

Several different people in the Bible are referred to as a "servant of God" or "God's servant" because of the loyal work they rendered for the Lord. But Jesus is the only person who deserves to be called God's "righteous servant."

This name for Jesus appears in one of the famous messianic "Servant Songs" of the prophet Isaiah. At the beginning of the Lord's public ministry, Matthew quoted this passage and identified Jesus as this person the prophet had predicted (Isaiah 42:1–4; Matthew 12:15–18). The servant's mission was being fulfilled through Jesus' teaching and healing ministry. He was the holy and righteous agent whom the Father sent on a mission of redemption into a dark and sinful world.

Jesus lived up to this name through His healing and teaching ministry. On one occasion His disciples began to argue over who would occupy the places of honor in His future glory. "Whosoever of you will be the chiefest, shall be servant of all," He gently reminded them. "For even the Son of man came not to be ministered unto, but to minister, and to give his life a ransom for many" (Mark 10:44–45).

Learn More: John 13:16 / Philippians 2:5–8

ROCK

There is none holy as the Lord:
for there is none beside thee:
neither is there any rock like our God.
1 Samuel 2:2

Hannah uttered this prayer when she brought her son Samuel to Eli the priest. God had answered her prayer for a son, and she followed through on her promise to devote him to the Lord. She had found the Lord to be the Rock, the strong and dependable One who answers the prayers of His people.

The imagery of God as a rock appears often in the book of Psalms. In a psalm attributed to David, he praised God for serving as his Rock of defense against the murderous schemes of King Saul. "The Lord is my rock, and my fortress, and my deliverer," he declared, "my God, my strength, in whom I will trust" (Psalm 18:2).

The word *rock* when used of God refers not to a small stone but to a massive outcropping of solid rock, such as that on a mountainside. These huge formations are common throughout the land of Israel. They remain from one generation to the next, just as God is the eternal, unmovable One who is not subject to the ravages of time. See also *Spiritual Rock*.

Learn More: 2 Samuel 22:47; 23:3 / Psalm 62:7; 94:22

ROOT AND OFFSPRING OF DAVID

I Jesus have sent mine angel to testify
unto you these things in the churches.
I am the root and the offspring of David,
and the bright and morning star.
REVELATION 22:16

Jesus used this name for Himself in the closing verses of the final chapter of the last book of the Bible. It's as if He seized the last opportunity to tell the world who He is and what His life and ministry are all about.

Notice the dual focus of this name—the *root* of David and the *offspring* of David. It summarizes His existence as the God-man, the One who is both fully human and fully divine.

Because Jesus is the divine Son who served as the agent of creation, He is David's creator, or root. But because he came to earth in human form, He is also David's descendant, or offspring—the Messiah from the line of David who reigns over the spiritual kingdom that He came to establish. Thus Jesus is both superior to David and the rightful heir to his throne.

During Jesus' earthly ministry, people often addressed Him as the "Son of David" (see, for example, Matthew 20:31). They recognized Him as the spiritual heir to God's promise that a descendant of David would always reign over His people (2 Samuel 7:16). See also *Son of David*.

Learn More: Isaiah 9:7; 11:1; 55:3 / Jeremiah 23:5

SAVIOUR

*And there is no God else beside me; a just God
and a Saviour; there is none beside me.*
ISAIAH 45:21

In the Bible, the name *Saviour* is applied to both God the
Father and God the Son. In this verse from the prophet
Isaiah, the Lord assured His people that He as their Savior
was the only true God. He demanded their loyalty and
obedience.

A savior is a person who rescues or delivers others
from danger. When this name is used of God in the Old
Testament, it usually refers to physical deliverance. The
supreme example of this was God's rescue of the Israelites
from Egyptian slavery. Acting as deliverer, God sent plagues
against the Egyptians until the pharaoh gave in and allowed
the people to leave his country.

God's role as a Savior reaches its full flower in the New
Testament. An angel told shepherds near Bethlehem when
Jesus was born, "I bring you good tidings of great joy, which
shall be to all people. For unto you is born this day in the
city of David a Saviour, which is Christ the Lord" (Luke
2:10–11). The shepherds were awestruck by the news that
this newborn baby was to be a Savior for God's people
(Luke 2:8–15).

Learn More: Ephesians 5:23 / 1 Timothy 4:10 / 1 John 4:14

SCEPTRE OUT OF ISRAEL

There shall come a Star out of Jacob,
and a Sceptre shall rise out of Israel,
and shall smite the corners of Moab, and
destroy all the children of Sheth.
NUMBERS 24:17

Balaam, a pagan wizard, was hired by the king of Moab to pronounce a curse against the Israelites. But the Lord led Balaam to *bless* the Israelites instead. In this verse, Balaam even prophesied that a "Sceptre. . .out of Israel," a strong leader, would rise up to crush the Moabites.

This verse is also considered a prophecy with a long-range fulfillment, referring to Jesus as the Savior-Messiah whom God would send to deliver His people.

A scepter was a short staff, similar to a walking stick, that symbolized the power and authority of a king. In the book of Esther, King Ahasuerus of Persia extended his royal scepter for Queen Esther to touch (Esther 5:2). This gave her permission to come into his presence and present her request to the king.

The imagery of a royal scepter as applied to Jesus symbolizes His power, authority, and universal dominion. In the book of Hebrews, God the Father declares to Jesus the Son, "Thy throne. . .is for ever and ever: a sceptre of righteousness is the sceptre of thy kingdom" (Hebrews 1:8).

Learn More: Genesis 49:10 / Esther 4:11 / Psalm 45:6 / Zechariah 10:11

SEED OF THE WOMAN

And I will put enmity between thee and
the woman, and between thy seed
and her seed; it shall bruise thy head,
and thou shalt bruise his heel.
GENESIS 3:15

God spoke these words to Satan in the garden of Eden after Satan had persuaded Adam and Eve to eat the forbidden fruit. This verse is known as the *protoevangelium*, a Latin word meaning "the first gospel."

It is called the first gospel because it contains the Bible's first prediction of the coming of Christ. Jesus is depicted as the "seed" of the woman, Eve. He will wage war against Satan's forces. Satan will manage to bruise Jesus' heel—a reference to the forces that executed Him on the cross. But Jesus will rise from the dead and deal a crushing blow to Satan's head. In the end time, Jesus will win the final victory over Satan and cast him into the lake of fire (Revelation 20:10).

This name may be a subtle reference to the virgin birth of Jesus. He was conceived in Mary's womb by the Holy Spirit, not by a human father. She was told by the angel Gabriel, "The Holy Ghost shall come upon thee, and the power of the Highest shall overshadow thee: therefore also that holy thing which shall be born of thee shall be called the Son of God" (Luke 1:35).

Learn More: Genesis 3:1 / Romans 3:23 / 1 Corinthians 15:45 / 1 Timothy 2:14

SEVEN SPIRITS

John to the seven churches which are in Asia:
Grace be unto you, and peace, from him which
is, and which was, and which is to come; and
from the seven Spirits which are before his
throne; and from Jesus Christ, who is the
faithful witness.
REVELATION 1:4–5

This reference to the Holy Spirit as "seven Spirits" is puzzling to many Bible students. We know from the apostle Paul's writings that the Holy Spirit is one. He declared to the believers at Corinth, "By one Spirit are we all baptized into one body" (1 Corinthians 12:13). So how could the apostle John in these verses from Revelation claim that the Holy Spirit is seven in number?

The best explanation is that John used the number seven to emphasize the fullness and completeness of the Holy Spirit. Seven was considered the perfect number in Bible times, and it appears often throughout the Bible to symbolize wholeness and perfection (see, for example, Deuteronomy 16:15; Matthew 18:21–22). John used the number in this sense many times throughout Revelation: seven candlesticks (1:12), seven stars (1:16), seven seals (5:1), seven horns and seven eyes (5:6).

Learn More: Genesis 33:3 / Job 2:13 / Psalm 12:6 / John 14:16

SHEPHERD

*The LORD is my shepherd; I shall not
want. He maketh me to lie down in
green pastures: he leadeth me beside
the still waters. He restoreth my soul.*
PSALM 23:1–3

This name of God is one of the favorites of Bible students,
perhaps because it occurs in one of the most familiar
passages of scripture—the Twenty-third Psalm. This psalm
has been called the "Shepherd Psalm" because of its
beautiful description of the Lord as the Shepherd of His
people.

David apparently wrote this psalm toward the end of
his life as he reflected how the Lord had been his never-
failing guide. Like a shepherd who leads his sheep to green
pastures and quiet streams for food and water, the Lord
had supplied David's needs. From his humble beginnings
as a shepherd boy, all the way to the throne of Israel, God
had blessed David with more than he deserved. David was
confident that God would continue to sustain him, even
as he walked "through the valley of the shadow of death"
(Psalm 23:4).

Like David, all of us need the divine Shepherd, who will
guide us throughout this life and beyond. What a blessing
it is to count ourselves as "the sheep of his pasture" (Psalm
100:3). See also *Good Shepherd*.

Learn More: Psalm 80:1 / Isaiah 40:11 / John 10:11 /
Hebrews 13:20

SHIELD

Let them also that love thy name
*be joyful in thee. For thou, L*ORD*,*
wilt bless the righteous; with favour
wilt thou compass him as with a shield.
PSALM 5:11–12

This verse is from a psalm of David in which he prayed for protection from his enemies. He used military terminology to characterize God as his "shield" who would surround him and absorb the blows of those who attacked.

The original Hebrew word in this verse refers to the large, full-body shield that warriors crouched behind. This protected them from soldiers with swords and spears, as well as from archers who were shooting arrows from a distance.

Another type of shield was the buckler. It was strapped to the arm for protection in hand-to-hand combat. The buckler as a metaphor for God's protection also appears in the Bible (Psalm 18:30).

The psalmist described the Lord's salvation as a shield (Psalm 18:35). In the New Testament, the apostle Paul urged believers to take up "the shield of faith, wherewith ye shall be able to quench all the fiery darts of the wicked" (Ephesians 6:16).

As our Shield, God assures our well-being in the midst of earthly trials and conflicts. He literally surrounds us with His watchful care.

Learn More: 2 Samuel 22:3 / Psalm 3:3; 84:9 / Proverbs 30:5

SHILOH

The sceptre shall not depart from Judah,
nor a lawgiver from between his feet,
until Shiloh come; and unto him shall
the gathering of the people be.
GENESIS 49:10

Genesis 49 contains the aging Jacob's blessings on his twelve sons, whose descendants would become the twelve tribes of Israel. This verse is part of his blessing of Judah, the tribe out of which the rulers of Israel would emerge, beginning with King David.

Shiloh is a Hebrew word meaning "the one to whom it belongs." Thus, Jacob was saying that Judah would wield the royal scepter of leadership in Israel until the one to whom the scepter belonged arrived on the scene. This is a veiled reference to the coming Messiah.

All authority and power belong to Jesus because God has delegated His jurisdiction over His people to His Son. Jesus is also deserving of all power because He rules in justice and righteousness. He will never use His power for anything but the good of His church and those who devote their lives to Him and His service.

No matter what happens to us in this life, we can rest safe and secure in the arms of Shiloh—the One who holds the whole world in His hands.

Learn More: Luke 4:36 / Colossians 1:16 /
Revelation 5:1–8

SON OF ABRAHAM

The book of the generation of Jesus Christ,
the son of David, the son of Abraham.

MATTHEW 1:1

Abraham was the father of the Jewish people. Many centuries before Jesus' time, God called Abraham to leave his home and family in Mesopotamia and move to the land of Canaan. Here God would begin to build a nation that would be His exclusive possession. He promised Abraham, "I will bless them that bless thee, and curse him that curseth thee: and in thee shall all families of the earth be blessed" (Genesis 12:3).

As the Son of Abraham, Jesus is the ultimate fulfillment of this promise, or covenant, that God made with Abraham. In His human lineage and by His nationality, Jesus was a Jew—the people whom God promised to bless above all the nations of the earth.

But God never intended for His promise of blessing to apply only to the Jewish people. He wanted to bless all nations through the influence of Abraham's offspring. When the Jews forgot this part of the covenant, God sent His Son Jesus to remind them that He had placed no limits on His love and grace. Jesus as the Son of Abraham fulfilled God's redemptive plan by coming as Savior for the entire world.

Learn More: Isaiah 42:6 / Matthew 28:19–20 /
Acts 3:13; 13:47

SON OF DAVID

The book of the generation of Jesus Christ,
the son of David, the son of Abraham.
MATTHEW 1:1

This name of Jesus appears in the very first verse of the New Testament for good reason. It expresses the truth that Jesus as the Son of David ties together the Old and New Testaments. The genealogies of Jesus in the Gospels of Matthew and Luke declare that Jesus in His human lineage was descended from David (Matthew 1:6; Luke 3:31). Thus, Jesus fulfilled God's promise to David that one of David's descendants would always reign over His people (2 Samuel 7:1–16; Psalm 132:11–12).

During Jesus' earthly ministry, those who sought Him out for healing often called Him by this name. For example, blind Bartimaeus of Jericho shouted to Him, "Jesus, thou son of David, have mercy on me" (Mark 10:47).

But Jesus never referred to Himself by this name. He may have avoided it because it tended to feed the expectation of the Jewish people that the Messiah would come as a political conqueror, not a spiritual Savior.

Learn More: Matthew 9:27; 12:23 / Luke 18:38 /
2 Timothy 2:8

SON OF GOD

Now when the centurion, and they that were with him, watching Jesus, saw the earthquake, and those things that were done, they feared greatly, saying, Truly this was the Son of God.
MATTHEW 27:54

This verse refers to the Roman military officer who presided over the execution of Jesus. He was so impressed with the miraculous signs at Jesus' death (Matthew 27:50–53) that he declared Jesus was none other than the Son of God.

This name emphasizes Jesus' divine nature and shows that He came to earth under the authority of God the Father on a mission of redemption. It also highlights Jesus' close, personal relationship with His heavenly Father. He knew God like no other person has ever known Him. He addressed God often in His prayers as "Father" (John 17:1–26).

Jesus as God's Son was perfectly obedient to His Father. He refused to be sidetracked by Satan's temptations at the beginning of His public ministry. His last words from the cross were "It is finished" (John 19:30). This was not the whimper of a dying man but a declaration of victory over the forces of sin and death. He accomplished the work that His Father commissioned Him to do. See also *Abba, Father.*

Learn More: Matthew 6:9; 14:33 / Luke 4:1–13 / Acts 9:20 / Romans 1:4

SON OF MAN

And Jesus said unto him, Foxes have holes,
and birds of the air have nests; but the Son
of man hath not where to lay his head.

LUKE 9:58

Jesus identified Himself by this name when He responded to a man who promised to become His disciple. He wanted this would-be follower to know that serving Him as the Son of man would require sacrifice.

This name occurs often in the Gospel narratives. Jesus used the title as a substitute for the first-person pronoun "I," as in the verse above. He called Himself the "Son of man" when predicting His suffering and death (Luke 9:22). And He also used it when referring to His authority and power, as in "the Son of man is Lord also of the sabbath" (Mark 2:28).

Jesus may have borrowed this name from the prophet Ezekiel. It appears many times throughout this Old Testament book. The basic meaning of *Son of man* is "mortal" or "human being." Perhaps Jesus preferred this title because it implied His total identification with humankind. The Son of man came to earth as a man—our brother and fellow sufferer—to deliver us from our bondage to sin. He summed up His mission of redemption in a few simple words: "The Son of man is come to seek and to save that which was lost" (Luke 19:10).

Learn More: Ezekiel 2:1; 11:2; 33:7

SON OF MARY

Is not this the carpenter, the son of Mary, the brother of James, and Joses, and of Juda, and Simon? . . . And they were offended at him.

MARK 6:3

The citizens of Nazareth could not believe the boy who had grown up among them was a prophet sent from God. They knew Him only as the carpenter and the "son of Mary."

The virgin Mary knew from the very beginning that her son was God's special gift to the world (Luke 1:26–38). But she apparently brought Him up like any normal Jewish boy (Luke 2:51–52). She had other children who were born by natural means after Jesus' miraculous conception (Mark 6:3). But Jesus as her firstborn son must have had a special place in her heart.

She knew about His special powers because she told the servants at a wedding feast where the wine had run out, "Whatsoever he saith unto you, do it" (John 2:5). Jesus responded by turning water into wine.

Did Mary realize that her son Jesus was destined to be executed like a common criminal? No one knows, but she was at the execution site when He was nailed to the cross. One of the last things Jesus did before He died was to make arrangements for the welfare of His mother (John 19:27).

Learn More: Matthew 1:18; 13:55 / Luke 1:26–30; 2:34 / Acts 1:14

SON OVER HIS OWN HOUSE

And Moses verily was faithful in all his house, as a servant, for a testimony of those things which were to be spoken after; but Christ as a son over his own house; whose house are we, if we hold fast the confidence and the rejoicing of the hope firm unto the end.

HEBREWS 3:5-6

The writer of Hebrews posed these verses as an argument that Jesus is superior to Moses, the great deliverer of God's people from slavery. Moses was faithful in his house, or the household of God's people of faith. But he was a mere *servant* in this house. By contrast, Jesus was a Son who *ruled over* His own house, or the church that He founded. So it follows logically that Jesus is superior to Moses.

This passage refers to a time in the wilderness when Moses' brother, Aaron, and his sister, Miriam, questioned his leadership. God stopped their rebellion by pointing out that Moses was His true prophet "who is faithful in all mine house" (Numbers 12:7).

But no matter how faithful Moses was to God, Jesus was even more so. He was God's own Son who gave His life to set people free from their bondage to sin. All believers are blessed by the faithfulness He demonstrated to God's redemptive plan.

Learn More: John 1:17; 6:32 / Hebrews 3:3

SPIRIT OF ADOPTION

*For ye have not received the spirit of bondage
again to fear; but ye have received the Spirit of
adoption, whereby we cry, Abba, Father.*

ROMANS 8:15

In this verse the apostle Paul contrasts the situation of a person before he becomes a believer to the new status he enjoys after his conversion. The old life is comparable to that of a slave in bondage who has no rights or privileges. But after being converted to new life in Christ, a person has all the advantages of sonship as a child of God the Father.

Paul used the concept of adoption to emphasize our new status with God. We were once children of sin, but God delivered us from our bondage and adopted us as His own. So close is our relationship to God as our adoptive Father that we can call Him *Abba*, an Aramaic word equivalent to our modern "Daddy" or "Papa."

The Holy Spirit has a vital role in this adoption process. His presence in our lives assures us that we belong to God. His Spirit will never let us forget that we enjoy a position of dignity and honor in the family of God the Father and Jesus the Son.

Learn More: Romans 8:23 / Galatians 4:5 / Ephesians 1:5

SPIRIT OF FAITH

*We having the same spirit of faith, according
as it is written, I believed, and therefore have I
spoken; we also believe, and therefore speak.*

2 CORINTHIANS 4:13

To understand these words from the apostle Paul, we must
consider his famous statement about the centrality of faith:
"For by grace are ye saved through faith; and that not of
yourselves: it is the gift of God: not of works, lest any man
should boast" (Ephesians 2:8–9).

Paul did not say that we are saved *by* faith, but *through*
faith. It is Christ's sacrifice on the cross that saves; we
claim this truth for ourselves by placing our faith in Him.
This is our human response to His sacrifice. Through faith in
Christ, we experience forgiveness for our sins and accept
Him as the Lord of our lives.

If human faith is an essential element of the salvation
process, how do we have such faith? Paul's answer is that
saving faith is a work of the Holy Spirit—the "spirit of faith."
He alone can convict us of sin and lead us to declare our
faith in Jesus Christ. Without the movement of the Holy
Spirit to kindle faith in our hearts and minds, we would
remain hopelessly lost in our sin.

Learn More: Romans 5:1 / 1 Corinthians 12:9 /
Galatians 3:14 / 2 Timothy 4:7

SPIRIT OF GLORY

*If ye be reproached for the name of Christ,
happy are ye; for the spirit of glory and of
God resteth upon you: on their part he is evil
spoken of, but on your part he is glorified.*

1 PETER 4:14

The apostle Peter in this verse may have been thinking back to the time when Jesus told the disciples what to do when they were persecuted for following Him. They were to "take no thought how or what ye shall speak: for it shall be given you in that same hour what ye shall speak. For it is not you that speak, but the Spirit of your Father which speaketh in you" (Matthew 10:19–20).

In effect, Jesus told the disciples not to retaliate against or resist their persecutors but to trust the Holy Spirit—the "spirit of glory"—to take care of them and give them the words to say in rebuttal. The same Spirit that guided Jesus throughout His ministry would also abide with them, strengthening them to serve as His bold witnesses.

The spirit of glory does not desert us during our times of persecution. He honors us for our sacrificial suffering in God's service, just as He glorified Jesus by raising Him from the dead (1 Peter 3:18).

Learn More: Ezekiel 43:5 / Ephesians 3:16 / 1 Peter 4:14

SPIRIT OF KNOWLEDGE AND THE FEAR OF THE LORD

And the spirit of the LORD shall rest upon him, the spirit of wisdom and understanding, the spirit of counsel and might, the spirit of knowledge and of the fear of the LORD.

ISAIAH 11:2

These two names of the Holy Spirit are among six that the prophet Isaiah used in this one verse. The prophet grouped these names together into three sets of two names each. He must have thought of these twin names as closely related to each other.

So how do the "spirit of knowledge" and the "spirit of the fear of the LORD" relate? Isaiah may have had in mind a well-known verse from the book of Proverbs: "The fear of the LORD is the beginning of knowledge" (Proverbs 1:7). "Fear of the Lord" means respect or reverence for God. So this proverb declares that a healthy respect for God is the most important attitude for a person to have as he accumulates the knowledge he needs to be happy and successful in life.

Through His Spirit, God plants in our hearts a reverence that leads us to honor Him in our lives. This is the foundation on which we build knowledge and understanding of Him and His work in the world.

Learn More: Daniel 5:12 / 1 Corinthians 12:8 / Ephesians 1:17

SPIRIT OF LIFE

For the law of the Spirit of life in
Christ Jesus hath made me free
from the law of sin and death.
ROMANS 8:2

This statement of the apostle Paul reminds us of another of his famous declarations about the Holy Spirit: "Where the Spirit of the Lord is, there is liberty" (2 Corinthians 3:17). By the "law of the Spirit of life" in the verse above, Paul means the principle by which the Holy Spirit operates.

Life in the Spirit gives us the power to live free from the bondage of sin and death. This does not mean that believers will never experience death, because physical death is the lot of every human being. Paul means that those who have accepted Jesus Christ as Savior and Lord are no longer in bondage to our sinful nature. Just as Jesus defeated death, He has promised that all believers will enjoy eternal life with Him.

As the Spirit of "life," the Holy Spirit shares this aspect with Jesus (John 11:25–26). Those who have Jesus and the Holy Spirit in their lives have no reason to fear the grave.

Learn More: Job 10:12; 33:4 / 2 Corinthians 3:6

SPIRIT OF PROPHECY

And I fell at his feet to worship him. And he said unto me, See thou do it not: I am thy fellowservant, and of thy brethren that have the testimony of Jesus: worship God: for the testimony of Jesus is the spirit of prophecy.

REVELATION 19:10

The apostle John, author of the book of Revelation, fell in awe before an angel at the throne of God. The angel told John not to worship him but to worship God and His Son, Jesus Christ. The angel went on to identify the Holy Spirit who bore witness of Jesus as the "spirit of prophecy."

The coming Messiah was often spoken of by the prophets of the Old Testament. This insight did not come to them through the power of their intellect but by direct revelation of God through the agency of His Holy Spirit.

These inspired prophecies were not restricted to the Old Testament. When Simeon saw the infant Jesus in the temple, he declared that the baby was the long-awaited Messiah whom God had finally sent to His people. This truth was revealed to Simeon by the Holy Spirit (Luke 2:25–27).

Learn More: Numbers 12:6 / Luke 7:16 / Acts 3:22 / 2 Peter 1:20

SPIRIT OF TRUTH

*Howbeit when he, the Spirit of truth,
is come, he will guide you into all truth.*
JOHN 16:13

Jesus told His disciples He would soon be leaving them to return to the Father. But they would continue to feel His presence through the operation of the "Spirit of truth" in their lives.

The word *truth* can refer to something that is enduring or authentic, in contrast to something that is temporary or of little value. This aspect of truth is what Jesus had in mind. His disciples would discover that the Spirit was enduring and dependable. He would never leave them. When all else disappeared, the Spirit would continue to infuse them with power.

Jesus also told His disciples that the Spirit of truth would help them continue to bear witness of Him (John 15:26). The memory of His physical presence would eventually grow dim in their minds. But the Holy Spirit would help them recall His life and teachings and pass these truths on to others.

All who follow Christ are beneficiaries of the faithful witness of the disciples and other early believers. They eventually wrote down their eyewitness accounts of Jesus' life and ministry. These narratives were passed on to future generations through the inspired writings of the New Testament.

Learn More: John 14:16–17; 15:26 / 1 John 4:6

SPIRIT OF WISDOM AND REVELATION

That the God of our Lord Jesus Christ, the Father of glory, may give unto you the spirit of wisdom and revelation in the knowledge of him.

EPHESIANS 1:17

This name of the Holy Spirit from the apostle Paul combines three important ingredients of the spiritual life—wisdom, revelation, and knowledge.

Revelation is the process by which God makes Himself known. Our human minds would know nothing about God unless He had chosen to reveal Himself to us. He has done this supremely through the written scriptures.

The writings that make up the Bible were revealed by God. But He inspired human beings through the activity of His Spirit to understand these divine messages and to write them down. Through the inspired scriptures, we gain knowledge about God—His nature as Creator, Sustainer, and Redeemer. But the Spirit teaches us more than factual information about God. We come to know Him in a personal sense as the God who loved us enough to send His own Son to save us from our sins.

Wisdom is the ability to apply what we know to real-life situations. The Holy Spirit gives us the wisdom to honor God in the way we live out our faith in the world.

Learn More: Deuteronomy 34:9 / Isaiah 11:2 / Acts 6:10 / 2 Peter 1:20–21

SPIRITUAL ROCK

All our fathers were under the cloud. . .
and did all drink the same spiritual drink:
for they drank of that spiritual Rock that
followed them: and that Rock was Christ.
1 CORINTHIANS 10:1, 4

These verses from the apostle Paul reminded the Jewish people of their years of wandering in the wilderness after their deliverance from slavery. God guided them with a cloud (Exodus 13:21), and He saved them from the Egyptian army at the Red Sea (Exodus 14:21–27).

In the barren wilderness, God also provided water for His people. It gushed from a rock when Moses struck it with his staff at God's command (Numbers 20:8–11). Paul picked up on this rock imagery and described Jesus as the "spiritual Rock" who meets the needs of God's people. Just as the rock in the desert was the source of water for the Israelites, Christ guides and protects those who place their trust in Him.

Was Jesus actually present with the Israelites in the wilderness? Paul declares that Christ their spiritual Rock "followed them." Or was Paul speaking metaphorically? We can't say for sure. But one thing we know for certain is that Jesus is a modern-day spiritual Rock who quenches our thirst and provides strength and stability for daily living. See also *Rock*.

Learn More: Exodus 17:6 / 1 Samuel 2:2 / Psalm 31:2; 62:6

STAR OUT OF JACOB

There shall come a Star out of Jacob,
and a Sceptre shall rise out of Israel,
and shall smite the corners of Moab, and
destroy all the children of Sheth.
NUMBERS 24:17

Balaam, a pagan magician, assigned this name to the coming Messiah. He would be a "Star out of Jacob" who would rule over His people with great power and authority.

The nation of Israel is sometimes referred to in the Bible as "Jacob" because it sprang from the twelve sons, or tribes, of the patriarch Jacob. A star was considered the symbol of an exceptional king. When Jesus was born in Bethlehem, a bright star appeared in the sky to mark the occasion. This star guided the wise men from the east to the place in Bethlehem where He was (Matthew 2:2–9).

The word *star* is tossed around loosely in our time. We have rock stars, movie stars, and superstars in every sport from baseball to wrestling. But the name of Jesus will live on long after these pseudostars have disappeared. He alone has the power to save and bring people into fellowship with God the Father. He reigns over His people as the Star that will never burn out. See also *Bright and Morning Star*; *Dayspring from on High*.

Learn More: Genesis 26:4 / Daniel 12:3 / 2 Peter 1:19 / Revelation 11:15; 22:16

STRENGTH

*The LORD is my strength and song, and he
is become my salvation: he is my God,
and I will prepare him an habitation;
my father's God, and I will exalt him.*
EXODUS 15:2

This verse is part of the passage of scripture known as the "Song of Moses" (Exodus 15:1–19). Moses led the Israelites to sing this praise to the Lord after He rescued them from the pursuing army of the Egyptian pharaoh at the Red Sea.

The people had witnessed the awesome power of the Lord as He divided the waters of the sea to give them safe passage. Even before this event, He had plagued the Egyptians again and again until Pharaoh allowed the Israelites to leave the country. No wonder Moses referred to this wonder-working God as his "strength."

In later years the Lord also provided a meal for the prophet Elijah that gave him strength to escape the plot of the wicked queen Jezebel (1 Kings 19:8).

There is no shortage of power in the God we serve. And He invites us to partake of His strength in our times of need. The prophet Isaiah declared, "He giveth power to the faint; and to them that have no might he increaseth strength" (Isaiah 40:29).

Learn More: Psalm 18:1–2; 19:14 / Jeremiah 16:19 / Habakkuk 3:19

STRONG TOWER

The name of the LORD is a strong tower:
the righteous runneth into it, and is safe.
PROVERBS 18:10

Towers were massive stone structures built above the defensive walls of ancient cities. From these elevated positions, defenders could shoot arrows or hurl stones on the enemy forces outside the wall. These towers also served as a final line of defense if the invading army should succeed in breaking through the wall or battering down the city gate.

The author of this proverb compared the Lord to one of these defensive towers. His righteous followers can seek safety and security in Him as the "strong tower." In a prayer of gratitude, King David expressed his praise to the Lord for serving as his "tower of salvation" against his enemies. The Lord "sheweth mercy to his anointed, unto David," he declared, "and to his seed for evermore" (2 Samuel 22:51).

The Lord used the imagery of a tower to assure the prophet Jeremiah that He would strengthen him for the task of delivering His unpopular message to the nation of Judah. "I have set thee for a tower and a fortress among my people," He told the prophet, "that thou mayest know and try their way" (Jeremiah 6:27). See also *Fortress*.

Learn More: 2 Samuel 22:3 / Psalm 18:2; 61:3; 144:2

TEACHER COME FROM GOD

*The same [Nicodemus] came to Jesus by
night, and said unto him, Rabbi, we know
that thou art a teacher come from God:
for no man can do these miracles that
thou doest, except God be with him.*

JOHN 3:2

Nicodemus was a respected Pharisee who recognized Jesus as a "teacher come from God." He wanted to learn more about Him and His teachings. So he came to talk with Jesus face to face.

In His role as teacher, Jesus communicated God's message to individuals like Nicodemus, as well as large groups of people (see Mark 4:1). He was also a patient teacher with His disciples, who were slow to understand His mission of redemptive suffering (Luke 24:45–47).

Jesus was an effective communicator of divine truth because of His teaching style. He did not focus on abstract theories but on down-to-earth truths that the common people could understand. He used objects from everyday life to connect with His audience.

But the most impressive thing about His teaching is that it was stamped with the power of God the Father. He made it clear that He spoke under authority from God Himself. The people "were astonished at his doctrine: for he taught them as one that had authority, and not as the scribes" (Mark 1:22).

Learn More: Proverbs 23:12 / Matthew 23:34 / Mark 12:37 / Luke 4:32 / 2 Timothy 3:16

TRUTH

*Jesus saith unto him [Thomas], I am
the way, the truth, and the life: no man
cometh unto the Father, but by me.*

JOHN 14:6

Jesus always spoke the truth to His followers. But beyond
saying the truth, He *was* and *is* the Truth—the ultimate
reality in the universe. This is the sense in which Jesus
referred to Himself as "the truth" in His conversation with
the disciple Thomas.

Our world has many different views of truth. Some
people think that money and possessions are the ultimate
goal of life. Others say learning or knowledge lead to
truth. Many believe that each person has to find truth for
himself by constructing it from his own life experiences.

These modern theories remind us of Pilate, the Roman
governor who pronounced the death sentence against
Jesus. When Jesus told him that He had come into the
world to "bear witness unto the truth," Pilate asked, "What
is truth?" (John 18:37–38). The Truth stood so close to
Pilate that he could reach out and touch it, but he missed
it because of his unbelief.

What a tragedy! And what an accurate picture of an
unbelieving world—the arena into which we as believers
are sent to bear witness of Him who is Truth (Mark 16:15).

Learn More: Psalm 25:5; 31:5 / Malachi 2:6 / John 8:32 /
Ephesians 4:21

VINE

I am the vine, ye are the branches:
He that abideth in me, and I in him,
the same bringeth forth much fruit:
for without me ye can do nothing.
JOHN 15:5

Jesus spoke these words to the disciples during the Last Supper, on the night of His arrest. He knew His followers would need to be firmly attached to Him as the vine in order to weather the crisis of His forthcoming execution and death.

The plant that Jesus referred to was a grapevine. It had one main stem with several smaller shoots or runners branching off in all directions. These smaller branches owed their lives to the main stem. With this imagery, Jesus emphasized that His disciples should stay attached to Him as their Lord and Savior. He as "the vine" would sustain and nourish them so they would bear "much fruit" in the days ahead.

The fruit Jesus mentioned probably referred to the witness they would bear for Him after His resurrection and ascension. Most of these disciples—His "branches"— did abandon Him when He was arrested and crucified (Matthew 26:56). But after His resurrection, they regained their courage and continued the work that Jesus had trained them to do (Acts 1:13–14; 2:42–43).

Learn More: Job 15:33 / Isaiah 5:1–2 / Ezekiel 17:8 / Hosea 10:1 / John 15:1–4

WALL OF FIRE

For I, saith the LORD, will be unto her
a wall of fire round about, and will
be the glory in the midst of her.
ZECHARIAH 2:5

This name of God appears only here in the Bible. The prophet Zechariah used it to describe God's protection of the city of Jerusalem after the exile. The city's defensive walls had been destroyed by the Babylonians several decades before; this meant the Jewish exiles who returned to Jerusalem were in a precarious position. But God promised to protect them by becoming a "wall of fire" around the city.

Fire is often associated in the Bible with God's presence and protection. For example, God appeared in a burning bush to call Moses to deliver the Israelites from slavery in Egypt (Exodus 3:2). During the Exodus, the Lord used a pillar of fire to protect the Israelites from the pursuing Egyptian army while the Israelites crossed the Red Sea (Exodus 14:24–25). Then He sent a pillar of fire at night to guide His people on their journey through the wilderness (Exodus 13:21).

God still serves as the protector of His people. We can declare in confidence with the psalmist, "My help cometh from the LORD, which made heaven and earth" (Psalm 121:2). See also *Consuming Fire*; *Refiner's Fire*.

Learn More: Exodus 24:17 / Psalm 78:21 / Daniel 3:20–26

WAY

*Jesus saith unto him [Thomas], I am the
way, the truth, and the life: no man
cometh unto the Father, but by me.*
JOHN 14:6

The disciple Thomas was puzzled by Jesus' statement that He would leave His followers soon after His resurrection (John 14:1–4). Thomas wanted to know how he and the other disciples could find Jesus after He left. Jesus assured Thomas that He was the only "way" to their eternal reward. Thomas didn't need to know every detail about this destination or how to get there.

This conversation has a valuable lesson for modern Christians. Sometimes our curiosity about heaven takes our eyes off the One who has promised to take us there. We wonder where heaven will be and what it will look like.

We don't know the answers to these questions. But we do have a grasp of the most important thing: Jesus is the only way to that wonderful place. He knows the way there, and we know Him as "the way." So we can relax and trust His promise: "There is more than enough room in my Father's home. . . . When everything is ready, I will come and get you, so that you will always be with me where I am" (John 14:2–3 NLT).

Learn More: Psalm 86:11; 119:1; 143:8

WORD

*In the beginning was the Word, and the Word
was with God, and the Word was God.*

JOHN 1:1

The prologue of John's Gospel (John 1:1–18), of which this verse is part, focuses on Jesus as the eternal Son who existed with God the Father before the creation of the world. The verse is an obvious reference to the first three words of the first book of the Bible, in Genesis 1:1.

Just as God was "in the beginning," so Jesus existed "in the beginning" (John 1:1) as the eternal Word. This Word, who assumed human form to make His dwelling among human beings (John 1:14), is comparable to the words that God used to speak the universe into being (Genesis 1:3).

Words are the primary units of language that enable humans to communicate with one another. In the same way, Jesus reveals the will and mind of God the Father to earthbound mortals.

The description of Jesus as "the Word" is unique to the apostle John's writings. In his first epistle, John declared, "There are three that bear record in heaven, the Father, the Word, and the Holy Ghost: and these three are one" (1 John 5:7). This leaves little doubt that John thought of Jesus as the Word who was the second person of the Trinity.

Learn More: Psalm 12:6; 33:6 / John 15:3 / Revelation 19:13